Examining the South China Sea Disputes

Papers from the Fifth Annual CSIS South China Sea Conference

EDITORS
Murray Hiebert
Phuong Nguyen
Gregory B. Poling

A Report of the CSIS Sumitro Chair for Southeast Asia Studies

September 2015

CSIS | CENTER FOR STRATEGIC & INTERNATIONAL STUDIES

ROWMAN & LITTLEFIELD

Lanham • Boulder • New York • London

About CSIS

For over 50 years, the Center for Strategic and International Studies (CSIS) has worked to develop solutions to the world's greatest policy challenges. Today, CSIS scholars are providing strategic insights and bipartisan policy solutions to help decisionmakers chart a course toward a better world.

CSIS is a nonprofit organization headquartered in Washington, D.C. The Center's 220 full-time staff and large network of affiliated scholars conduct research and analysis and develop policy initiatives that look into the future and anticipate change.

Founded at the height of the Cold War by David M. Abshire and Admiral Arleigh Burke, CSIS was dedicated to finding ways to sustain American prominence and prosperity as a force for good in the world. Since 1962, CSIS has become one of the world's preeminent international institutions focused on defense and security; regional stability; and transnational challenges ranging from energy and climate to global health and economic integration.

Former U.S. senator Sam Nunn has chaired the CSIS Board of Trustees since 1999. Former deputy secretary of defense John J. Hamre became the Center's president and chief executive officer in 2000.

CSIS does not take specific policy positions; accordingly, all views expressed herein should be understood to be solely those of the author(s).

Acknowledgments

This report is made possible by general support to CSIS. No direct sponsorship contributed to its publication.

ISBN: 978-1-4422-5894-5 (pb); 978-1-4422-5895-2 (eBook)

Center for Strategic & International Studies
1616 Rhode Island Avenue, NW
Washington, DC 20036
202-887-0200 | www.csis.org

Rowman & Littlefield
4501 Forbes Boulevard
Lanham, MD 20706
301-459-3366 | www.rowman.com

Contents

Preface

The Center for Strategic and International Studies (CSIS) hosted its fifth annual South China Sea conference on July 21, 2015. The day featured keynote speeches by Representative Randy Forbes (R-VA), the chairman of the Subcommittee on Seapower and Projection Forces of the U.S. House Armed Services Committee, and Daniel Russel, assistant secretary of state for East Asian and Pacific Affairs. It wrapped up with a crisis simulation featuring top former U.S. officials, which gave the audience a window into the decisionmaking process in Washington that could kick into gear in case of a serious incident in the South China Sea.

But the bulk of the day was spent on discussions by an all-star lineup of South China Sea and legal experts, including representatives from Australia, China, the Philippines, the United Kingdom, the United States, and Vietnam. This report contains papers by nine of those experts, highlighting the diversity of views presented at the conference.

Each of the papers reflect the panels on which the authors spoke. Bill Hayton, Bonnie Glaser, and Wu Shicun discuss recent developments in the South China Sea. Pham Lan Dung (along with her coauthor Tran Huu Duy Minh) explores legal issues surrounding the disputes. Ian Storey, Patrick Cronin, Renato Cruz de Castro, and Peter Jennings examine various aspects of the military balance and regional order.

The papers that follow represent the views of the authors and do not reflect those of CSIS or the Sumitro Chair for Southeast Asia Studies.

1 The Impact of Strategic Balance in East Asia on a Small Power's Defense Policy

The Case of the Philippines in the Face of the South China Sea Dispute

Renato Cruz de Castro

The South China Sea is a semi-enclosed sea surrounded by China and several small and militarily weak Southeast Asian powers such as Brunei, Malaysia, the Philippines, and Vietnam. For almost three decades, these littoral states have been involved in a chronic competition, as they each seek to extend their sovereignty and jurisdictional claims over more than a hundred islets, reefs, and rocks and their surrounding waters. The dispute became dormant in the late 1990s and the early twenty-first century, after China and the Association of Southeast Asian Nations (ASEAN) signed the 2002 Declaration on the Conduct of Parties in the South China Sea.

However, tensions arose again in 2009 when China discarded its tactic of delaying the resolution of the dispute and instead began to assert its sovereignty over the contested waters. This shift in diplomatic tactics is aimed to deter other claimant states such as the Philippines and Vietnam from cementing their claims and to enable China to negotiate with these small powers from a position of strength. In an assertive posture, China consolidated its jurisdictional claims in the South China Sea by expanding its military reach and pursuing coercive diplomacy against other claimant states.[1] For instance, it increased naval patrols (using submarines, survey ships, and surface combatants) in Japan's exclusive economic zone (EEZ) and territorial waters, and intimidated foreign oil companies that tried to operate in the South China Sea.[2] Chinese leaders feel confident that with its political and economic clout and a strong People's Liberation Army (PLA), China can boldly advance its "core interests" in the maritime domain. This thrust is reflected by China's insistence on an air defense identification zone (ADIZ) in the East China Sea, the conduct of

1. Clive Schofield and Ian Storey, *The South China Sea Dispute: Increasing Stakes and Rising Tensions* (Washington DC: Jamestown Foundation, 2009), 1.
2. Michael A. Glosny "Getting Beyond Taiwan? Chinese Foreign Policy and PLA Modernization," *Strategic Forum* 261 (January 2011): 5.

live-fire exercises by the People's Liberation Army Navy (PLAN) and the People's Liberation Air Force in the Western Pacific, and the hard-line response of the PLAN and other maritime law enforcement agencies during several confrontations with Philippine and Vietnamese civilian ships in the South China Sea.[3]

Early on, this maritime dispute caught the attention of the United States, which is determined to maintain its naval primacy in East Asia in light of China's emergence as an economic and military power. In 2010 the United States declared that it is in its vital interests to maintain the freedom of navigation in the South China Sea and see the disputes be peacefully resolved through multilateralism and international law. In 2011 the administration of President Barack Obama announced the U.S. strategic rebalancing to the Asia-Pacific region. The move was made in part to ensure that the U.S. vision of a comprehensive rules-based system in the Asia Pacific will be backed by U.S. military power, and will apply to the resolution of clashing claims in the South China Sea.[4]

Interestingly Japan has also become interested in the South China Sea dispute. As China's geostrategic rival and a key U.S. ally in East Asia, Japan is bent on playing a balancing role in the dispute by helping other claimant states build up their respective naval capabilities.

The growing involvement of the United States and Japan in the South China Sea dispute has generated a strategic balance in the region. This situation enables these two naval powers to demonstrate their maritime prowess by drawing on their long-range surveillance and strike capabilities to maintain their "forces over-horizon" and power projections against an expansionist China in the South China Sea.[5] Alarmed by the PLAN's actions in the contested sea, the United States, with the support of Japan and other allies, has stepped up displays of its naval and air power and is determined to prevent China from establishing its primacy in the region.[6]

Consequently many international relations scholars and analysts have elevated the South China Sea dispute from a simple territorial row to a high-level geopolitical concern, deciding the disputed area is "a dangerous ground" or a "future of conflict."[7] As such, the South China Sea has become an arena where states with powerful navies will jockey for

---

3. National Institute for Defense Studies, *NIDS China Security Report 2014: Diversification of Roles in the People's Liberation Army and the People's Armed Police* (Tokyo: National Institute for Defense Studies, 2015), 3.

4. See Mark E. Manyin et al., "Pivot to the Pacific? The Obama Administration's 'Rebalancing' toward Asia," CRS Report R42448, March 28, 2012, https://www.fas.org/sgp/crs/natsec/R42448.pdf.

5. Malcolm Cook, Raoul Heinrichs, Rory Medcalf, and Andrew Shearer, *Power and Choice: Asian Security Futures* (Sydney: Lowy Institute, June 2010), 36.

6. Ibid., 33.

7. See Carlyle A. Thayer, "China's New Wave of Aggressive Assertiveness in the South China Sea," *International Journal of China Studies* 2, no. 3 (2011): 555–583; Taylor M. Fravel, "China's Strategy in the South China Sea," *Contemporary Southeast Asia* 33, no. 3 (2011): 292–319; Huai-Feng Ren and Fu-Kuo-Liu, "Transitional Security Pattern in the South China Sea and the Involvement of External Parties," *Issues and Studies* 49, no. 2 (2013): 103–145; Leszek Buszynski, "The South China Sea Maritime Dispute: Legality, Power, and Conflict Prevention," *Asian Journal of Peacebuilding* 1, no. 1 (2013): 39–63; and David Scott, "Conflict Irresolution in the South China Sea," *Asian Survey* 56, no. 6 (November/December 2012): 1019–1042.

strategic and diplomatic leverages with their warships in the high seas, pursue their conflicting claims for natural resources, and strive for supremacy in the Western Pacific.[8]

Trapped in this potentially dangerous strategic balance in East Asia are the small claimant states—Brunei, Malaysia, the Philippines, and Vietnam. Two of them, the Philippines and Vietnam, find themselves in a classic security dilemma, in which actions by China—the most powerful claimant state in the dispute—are viewed as extremely threatening by the other claimants.[9] They fear that China might seize some of the disputed features in the South China Sea given the potential energy reserves of these maritime territories, and their importance to maritime trade and as sea lanes of communication (SLOC).[10] Confronted by China's preponderant economic and military power, the two Southeast Asian states had no other recourse but to pursue a regional balance of power where the United States remains a resident Pacific power and a major twenty-first century strategic player. Such policy puts these two small powers squarely in the middle of a strategic standoff between China on one side and the United States and Japan on the other, which can ignite into a major conflict in the twenty-first century.

Using the Philippines as a case study, this paper examines how a small power responds and adjusts to a fluid and potentially dangerous strategic balance generated by mistrust, suspicion, and rivalry between China and the U.S./Japan tandem over a maritime dispute. It raises the main question: How does the Philippines adjust to this balance of power situation created by the involvement of these three major naval powers in the South China Sea dispute? It also explores four corollary questions:

1. What major developments led to the emergence of this fluid strategic balance of power in East Asia?
2. How do these three naval powers pursue their respective strategic interests in the dispute?
3. What are the characteristics of this strategic balancing by the three naval powers in East Asia?
4. How does the Philippines view this fluid and potentially dangerous strategic balance of power in the region?

China's Realpolitik Approach

Among the claimant states, China poses the biggest challenge to any efforts to either resolve/manage or escalate the South China Sea dispute and the tension associated with it.[11]

---

8. See Robert Kaplan, "The South China Sea is the Future of Conflict," *Foreign Policy*, August 15, 2011, 76–88.
9. Fravel, "China's Strategy in the South China Sea," 296.
10. Glosny, "Getting Beyond Taiwan," 4.
11. Alice D. Ba, "Staking Claims and Making Waves in the South China Sea: How Troubled Are the Waters?," *Contemporary Southeast Asia* 33, no. 3 (2011): 269.

Needless to say, China is the largest and most powerful of the littoral states, and it has established sovereign control over the southernmost islands of Hainan and the Paracel Islands in the South China Sea. It has also declared full sovereignty over most of the contested sea based on an old official Chinese map featuring a nine-dash line that extends as far south as the northern Malaysian and Bruneian coasts.[12] China views the consolidation of its claim over the South China Sea as contributing to its territorial integrity and national security. Nevertheless, from the viewpoint of the small Southeast Asian states, this is an ominous act of Chinese expansionism in a key strategic location with potential economic resources.[13]

Since the mid-1990s, China has developed an arsenal of conventional yet inexpensive and highly precise armed ballistic and cruise missiles aimed at virtually every U.S. air base and port in the Western Pacific. These weapons are also designed to sink enemy surface vessels (including U.S. aircraft carriers) operating hundreds of miles off China's coastal areas.[14] Chinese planners believe that their missiles, with anti-access/area denial (A2/AD) capabilities, can adequately prevent the U.S. Navy from intervening in China's conflicts with its neighbors or provoking a confrontation with China in the region.[15] Thus, the United States has reasons to believe that the PLAN has been developing strategies and weapon systems that can disrupt American naval and air operations or slow down the deployment of its air and naval forces to the theater of operations.[16]

Heading into the second decade of the twenty-first century, the South China Sea is now a focal point of U.S.-China strategic rivalry. The stretch of maritime territory from the Yellow Sea through the East China Sea, and down to the Strait of Taiwan toward the South China Sea is known as the first island chain (mainland Japan–Okinawa–the Philippines) that forms the front line of China's naval defense. By dominating these seas, China can extend its security perimeter and reinforce its influence over these crucial sea lanes of communication linking the Indian and Pacific Oceans. However, U.S. naval presence in the Western Pacific prevents China's reunification with Taiwan, and imperils its extended maritime trade routes and energy supply lines from the Middle East.[17]

With a booming economy and a formidable navy, China no longer focuses on preempting possible U.S. intervention in a Taiwan Strait crisis, but rather on denying the U.S. Navy access to the East China Sea and South China Sea or inside the first island chain. China has had an annual double-digit increase in defense spending since 2006. Consequently, in the past few years, the PLAN has acquired a growing fleet of Russian-made diesel-electric *Kilo*-class submarines and *Sovremenny*-class destroyers, along with several types of

12. Marc Lanteigne, *Chinese Foreign Policy: An Introduction* (New York: Routledge, 2009), 121.

13. David Scott, *China Stands Up: The PRC and the International System* (New York: Routledge, 2007), 104.

14. Aaron L. Friedberg, "Buckling Beijing: An Alternative U.S. China Policy," *Foreign Affairs* 91, no. 5 (September/October 2012): 53.

15. Ibid.

16. Roger Cliff, Mark Burles, Michael S. Chase, Derek Eaton, and Kevin L. Pollpeter, *Entering the Dragon's Lair: Chinese Antiaccess Strategies and Their Implications for the United States* (Santa Monica, CA: RAND, 2007), xvii.

17. Buszynski, "The South China Sea Maritime Dispute," 39.

indigenous-built destroyers, frigates, and nuclear-powered attack submarines. The PLAN has also upgraded its operational capabilities across the waters surrounding Taiwan and has deployed two new classes of ballistic and attack submarines. Moving beyond its strategic preoccupation on the Taiwan Strait, China's naval forces can generate regional tension by challenging the claims of smaller neighboring states, and in the long run change the strategic pattern of the maritime commons of East Asia and the Western Pacific, gradually easing out the U.S. Navy. Interestingly, Chinese media commentators have repeatedly emphasized the significance of China's blue-water navy and the exigency of protecting its territorial claims in the South China Sea.

With it naval prowess, China has become more assertive in the South China Sea. In March 2009 Chinese naval and fishing vessels harassed the USS *Impeccable*, which was openly conducting surveying operations in the South China Sea. The following year China warned the United States to respect its extensive maritime claims. In March 2010 Chinese officials told two visiting State Department senior officials that China would not tolerate any U.S. interference in the South China Sea, which is now part of its "core interests," on par with Taiwan and Tibet.[18] In 2011 the Chinese government increased its defense budget by 13 percent, in the hopes of boosting the PLAN's capability to accomplish a range of military functions including "winning local wars under information age conditions."[19]

Judging from its recent behavior, China's aggressive pursuit of claims in the South China Sea has increased in tandem with the expansion of its navy and maritime services.[20] It now conducts regular naval exercises that utilize modern surface combatants and even submarines.[21] These activities reflect China's intention to unilaterally and militarily resolve maritime disputes, flaunt its naval capabilities, and impress upon the other claimant states its de facto ownership of disputed territories.[22] In the long run China's naval capabilities will be directed not only to expand its maritime domain but also to deny foreign navies—especially that of the United States—access to the East and South China Seas. In time, it will be capable of depriving the U.S. 7th Fleet access to the Western Pacific inside the so-called first island chain.[23]

Apparently, with its naval prowess China is convinced that it can resolve its territorial row with the small claimant states according to its own terms. It can also relay an implicit message to the U.S. Navy to steer clear of the South China Sea and other contested maritime areas around China's periphery. Its naval buildup, along with other realpolitik tactics, has

---

18. Edward Wong, "China Asserts Role as a Naval Power," *International Herald Tribune*, April 23, 2010.

19. Jeremy Page, Jason Dean, and Julean E. Barnes, "Beijing's Buildup Stirs Fears," *Wall Street Journal*, March 5, 2011, http://www.wsj.com/articles/SB10001424052748703580004576180482219510892.

20. Peter Dutton, "Three Disputes and Three Objectives: China and the South China Sea," *Naval War College Review* 64, 4 (2011): 6.

21. For details on China's training exercises in its surrounding waters, see National Institute for Defense Studies, *NIDS China Security Report 2011* (Tokyo: National Institute for Defense Studies, 2011), 14–21.

22. See International Institute for Strategic Studies, *The Military Balance 2011: The Annual Assessment of Global Military Capabilities and Defence Economics* (London: International Institute for Strategic Studies, 2011), 196.

23. Yoichi Kato, "China's Naval Expansion in the Western Pacific," *Global Asia* 5, no. 4 (2010): 19.

resulted in a tense situation, and sometimes crises. Nevertheless, China's assertive power-based approach in imposing its claims over the South China Sea has rekindled U.S. strategic attention to and interest in the dispute.[24] When push comes to shove, China's use of force against any of the claimant states in the South China Sea dispute will generate two perceptions among Southeast Asian countries: that China is challenging U.S. naval supremacy in East Asia, and that an armed clash in the South China Sea will determine the future security dynamics of the region.

To avoid extremely provocative naval deployment, China assigns the regular patrolling of politically sensitive waters and land features to the vessels and aircraft to the China Coast Guard, which is under the command of the State Oceanic Administration. The coast guard was formed in 2013 to integrate several four previously independent civilian agencies: China Marine Surveillance, Maritime Border Police, Fishing Regulation Administration, and the General Administration of Customs. These civilian vessels have three tasks:

1. To challenge and detain fishing boats from other littoral states.
2. To explore and identify sites for Chinese oil drilling in the disputed waters.
3. To prevent other claimant states from deploying their seismic ships in energy-rich areas of the South China Sea.

All of these efforts target one specific objective in the South China Sea: "to change the (territorial) status quo by force based on Chinese assertion, which is incompatible with the existing order of international law."[25]

In mid-2012 China engaged the Philippines in a tense, two-month standoff at Scarborough Shoal using civilian and fishing vessels supported by the PLAN. During the stalemate, China stood its ground and insisted on its authority and control over the contested territory and its related resources and rights. A few days after Chinese and Filipino civilian vessels withdrew from the contested shoal, thus ending the impasse, China deployed military and paramilitary forces in the South China Sea. It took certain measures to advance its right to exploit marine and oil resources rights; strengthened its administrative control over the disputed land features; and ignored harsh criticisms from the United States, Japan, and other states.[26]

In September 2012 China created a new administration unit for the 1,100 Chinese citizens living on the island groups of the Spratlys, Paracels, and Macclesfield Bank/Scarborough Shoal. In addition, the Central Military Commission, China's most powerful military body, approved the stationing of PLA personnel to guard these islands. These actions were designed to reinforce China's territorial claims over the South China Sea. No less than

24. Dutton, "Three Disputes and Three Objectives," 9–11.

25. National Institute for Defense Studies, *NIDS China Security Report 2013* (Tokyo: National Institute for Defense Studies, 2014), 2.

26. Robert Sutter and Chin-hao Huang, "China-Southeast Asia Relations: Beijing Shifts to the Positive, Downplays Disputes," *Comparative Connections*, January 2014, http://csis.org/files/publication/1303qchina_seasia.pdf.

the president of the National Institute of South China Sea Studies based in Hainan Island admitted that the goal of the strategic move is to allow Beijing to "exercise sovereignty over all land features inside the South China Sea, including more than 40 islands now illegally occupied by Vietnam, the Philippines, and Malaysia."[27]

Interestingly, China sees itself as an actor committed to a peaceful settlement of the territorial row through diplomatic means. In its one-sided narrative, China insists that it always displays a restrained and constructive attitude, and is resolute to settling the South China Sea dispute.[28] The crux of the matter is that China seeks ways that are predicated on or preconditioned by bilateralism. Although China has acceded to a joint declaration with ASEAN on maintaining the status quo in the South China Sea, it prefers to engage the other claimant states in bilateral negotiations that preempt any third-party adjudication through the United Nations Convention on the Law of the Sea (UNCLOS) or any international organizations. Going further, it is unbending in its resolve to settle the issue by flexing its military muscles.

The Strategic Rebalancing and Changing U.S. Defense Strategy

During the ASEAN Regional Forum in Hanoi on July 20, 2010, U.S. secretary of state Hillary Clinton stated that it is vital to U.S. interests that the freedom of navigation, an open access to Asia's maritime commons, and the littoral states' respect for international maritime law in the South China Sea are respected. She mentioned the United States' preparedness to facilitate multilateral negotiations to settle the dispute over the Spratly Islands. In November 2011 the Obama administration announced a strategic "pivot" to the Asia-Pacific region. Accordingly, this refocusing of U.S. strategic attention to the Asia Pacific is to ensure "the United States will play a larger and long-term role in shaping this region and its future."[29] The main gambit is buttressed by U.S. diplomatic strategy of constraining China with a stick. This strategy does not involve a Cold War–style containment of China, which would be too simplistic, but rather to make China acknowledge "America's strength, determination, and strategy."[30] Its ultimate goal is to shape the norms and rules of the Asia-Pacific region and to ensure that "international law and norms be respected, that commerce and freedom of navigation are not impeded, that emerging powers build trust with their neighbors, and that disagreements are resolved peacefully without threats of coercion."[31]

27. Jane Perlez, "Philippines and China Ease Tensions in Rift at Sea," *New York Times*, June 18, 2012, http://www.nytimes.com/2012/06/19/world/asia/beijing-and-manila-ease-tensions-in-south-china-sea.html.
28. "Article Cites Historical Arguments to Defend China's Stance on Spratly Islands," BBC Monitoring Asia-Pacific, August 14, 2011.
29. White House Office of the Press Secretary, "Remarks by President Obama to the Australian Parliament," November 17, 2011.
30. Mark Landler, "Obama's Journey to Tougher Tack on a Rising China," *New York Times*, September 12, 2012, http://www.nytimes.com/2012/09/21/us/politics/obamas-evolution-to-a-tougher-line-on-china.html?_r=0.
31. Manyin et al., "Pivot to the Pacific," 1.

The U.S. strategic rebalancing to the Asia Pacific entails two interconnected strategic efforts: a geographical rebalancing of the United States' global priority from the Middle East and South Asia to the Asia Pacific, and veering away from the army-oriented, expensive, and troop-intensive counterinsurgency campaign toward the development of U.S. technological capability and edge in air and naval warfare.[32] Despite the downsides on U.S. ground troops and their counterinsurgency operations, these courses of action present three main advantages:

1. Continued U.S. involvement in global security affairs, notwithstanding the strategic pivot to the Asia Pacific, where U.S. economic and security interests are linked to the region's growth and dynamism.[33]
2. The end of the U.S. Army's and Marine Corps' large-scale counterinsurgency campaigns that have preoccupied the U.S. military since 2001, but the continued operations and maintenance of the U.S. Navy's 11 aircraft carriers.
3. Less investment on new weapons systems—such as the joint strike jet fighter, defense and offense in cyberspace, high-tech arms and equipment for special operations forces, existing nuclear forces, and the broad area of intelligence, surveillance, and reconnaissance—and more resources to achieve air and naval superiority.[34]

Accordingly, with these new technologies, the U.S. Navy and Air Force can counter China and Iran's ability to incapacitate U.S. power projection near their shores or airspaces, through cyberwarfare, ballistic and cruise missiles, and advanced air defenses.[35] Hence the U.S. military must invest heavily in technology to neutralize or disable China's new asymmetric capabilities.

In June 2012 U.S. defense secretary Leon Panetta detailed the U.S. pivot to the Asia Pacific during the Shangri-La Dialogue in Singapore. He revealed that the U.S. Navy would have shifted 60 percent of its maritime assets to the Pacific by 2020. This strategic maneuver involves the deployment of six aircraft carriers, a majority of the navy's cruisers, destroyers, and littoral ships designed to operate closely offshore.[36] The United States also needs to preposition highly advanced war materiel such as the F-22 Raptor fighter jets, *Virginia*-class fast-attack submarines, lightly armed but fast littoral combat ships (LCSs), and a new class of destroyers labeled DDG-1000, improved precision-guided weapons, and new electronic warfare communication systems. Panetta added that the U.S. military is

32. Thomas Fargo, "The Military Side of Strategic Rebalancing," in *Asia Policy 14: Turning to the Pacific: U.S. Strategic Rebalancing toward Asia* (Washington, DC: National Bureau of Asian Research, 2012), 27–28.

33. Jim Lobe, "Less Counter-Insurgency, More Asia in New U.S. Strategy," Inter Press Service, January 5, 2012, http://www.ipsnews.net/2012/01/less-counter-insurgency-more-asia-in-new-us-strategy/.

34. Thom Shanker and Elizabeth Bumiller, "Obama Puts His Stamp on Strategy for a Leaner Military," *New York Times*, January 5, 2012, http://www.nytimes.com/2012/01/06/us/obama-at-pentagon-to-outline-cuts-and-strategic-shifts.html.

35. "President Obama Unveils Leaner Pentagon Budget: The Navy is Expected to Keep its Current Fleet of 11 Aircraft Carriers," *Herald Business Journal* (Everett, WA), January 6, 2012, http://www.theheraldbusinessjournal.com/apps/pbcs.dll/article?AID=/20120106/NEWS02/701069896/1052&template=PrinterFriendly.

36. Jane Perlez, "U.S. Gives Explanation for its 'Pivot' to Asia," *International Herald Tribune*, June 4, 2012, https://www.questia.com/newspaper/1P2-36286413/u-s-gives-explanation-for-its-pivot-to-asia.

also developing new weapon systems such as an aerial-refueling tanker, a bomber, and an aircraft for anti-submarine warfare to provide U.S forces with "the freedom of maneuver in areas where their access and freedom of action may be threatened."[37]

The global restructuring of U.S. naval and air assets to the Pacific will give teeth to the Pentagon's air/sea battle concept announced in 2010. The concept projects that in the unthinkable case of a war with China, U.S. armed forces will use combined air and naval forces to override or deter China's A2/AD systems within the first island chain. Similarly, it envisions U.S. air and naval units attacking Chinese surveillance and integrated air defense systems, followed by a weighted campaign to bomb Chinese land-based ballistic and anti-ship missile systems to "seize and sustain the initiative in air, sea, space, and cyber domains."[38] As an operational concept, the concept proposes the development of a new generation of naval and air weapon systems, as well as deeper military commitments of U.S. allies along East Asia's northern and southern coasts close to the South China Sea, namely Japan, Australia, South Korea, and the Philippines. A new and evolving U.S. strategy even presupposes neutralizing China's capability to control the air and sea around the first island chain. It requires the United States to integrate allied battle networks and strengthen allied capabilities by deploying U.S. ground troops as well as air and naval forces along the first island chain to deny the PLAN the sea control it needs to mount offensive operations against these islands.[39]

Extending the Sino-Japanese Rivalry into Southeast Asia

Since the mid-1990s, Japan has closely monitored the PLAN's buildup and sporadic flaunting of its naval prowess.[40] At present, the country is entangled in the South China Sea dispute, although it had no direct interests in the dispute initially. Katsuya Okada, a former Japanese foreign minister, commented in July 2010 that the unstable situation in the South China Sea could hamper Japan's trade and threaten regional peace.[41] In 2012 the National Institute for Defense Studies (NIDS) in Tokyo noted in its *China Security Report*, "Being in dispute with China over the EEZ and the boundary of the continental shelf in the East China Sea, Japan inevitably has to pay attention to China's action in the South China Sea."[42]

---

37. David S. Cloud, "Panetta Explains Pentagon's Pivot toward Asia," *Los Angeles Times*, June 1, 2012, http://latimesblogs.latimes.com/world_now/2012/06/panetta-explains-pentagon-pivot-toward-asia-.html.
38. T. X. Hammes and R. D. Hooker, "America's Ultimate Strategy in a Clash with China," *National Interest*, June 10, 2014, http://nationalinterest.org/feature/americas-ultimate-strategy-clash-china-10633.
39. Andrew F. Krepinevich Jr., "How to Deter China: The Case of Archipelagic Defense," *Foreign Affairs* 94, no. 2 (March/April 2015): 78–86.
40. National Institute for Defense Studies, *NIDS China Security Report 2011*, 17.
41. "Japanese FM Airs Concern over Territorial Disputes in South China Sea," BBC Monitoring Asia Pacific, July 27, 2010.
42. National Institute for Defense Studies, *NIDS China Security Report 2012* (Tokyo: National Institute for Defense Studies, 2012), 26.

There are two other reasons why the South China Sea dispute worries Japan. First, if China succeeds in intimidating the small littoral Southeast Asian states, it could use the same gambit in the East China Sea, where Japan has staked a claim to the Senkaku Islands.[43] Second, control of the South China Sea and the East China Sea is part of China's strategy of depriving the U.S. Navy access to China's surrounding waters, and giving the PLAN ingress to the Western Pacific outside of the first island chain.[44] If the U.S. Navy is driven out of the western part of the Pacific, the PLAN can easily dominate the South China Sea because even the combined navies of the Southeast Asian claimant states cannot match Chinese naval prowess.[45] Tokyo wants to preempt Beijing's calculation that should Chinese belligerence put an end to the South China Sea dispute, it can use the same methods to resolve the rivalry with Japan over the Senkaku Islands in the East China Sea.

The U.S. pivot to Asia provides further impetus for Japan to balance China in the contested sea. It entails a strong U.S. presence in Japan and South Korea, which is the cornerstone of the strategy, even as the United States enhances its security relationship with other states in and around Southeast Asia.[46] On many occasions, U.S. officials underscored that the freedom of navigation in the South China Sea can only be guaranteed if the disputed waters remain part of the global commons, that is, the South China Sea belongs to all states and is not subject to the sovereign control of a single powerful regional state. Hence, the Obama administration has supported the building of a coalition of states to constrain China's expansionism in the South China Sea. To complement U.S. efforts, Japan has forged separate defense partnerships and naval exchanges, specifically with Vietnam and the Philippines.[47] It has also provided coast guard vessels and training to both countries to boost their ability to patrol their respective maritime territories.

More significantly, Prime Minister Shinzo Abe continues to push for the reinterpretation of Article 9, known as the Peace Clause, of the 1947 Japanese constitution to enable the Self-Defense Forces (SDF) to exercise the right of "collective self-defense." A loose interpretation of this vague provision will allow the SDF to come to the aid of Japan's security partners that are under armed attack by a third party. Japan's modern and relatively large Maritime Self-Defense Force (MSDF), a fleet of six Aegis combat system–equipped destroyers with 39 guided-missile destroyers and 16 conventional submarines, can fill the strategic gap in the South China Sea. The MSDF can be supported by the Air Self-Defense Force (ASDF) with its expanding operational reach made possible by the development of mid-air refueling capacity and the acquisition of the Boeing KC-767 tanker. The International Institute for Strategic Studies (IISS) observes that Japan's national defense program guidelines for 2011–2015 contain reform measures enabling the SDF to respond to the shifting

43. Ian Storey, "Japan Steps Up to the South China Sea Plate: Tokyo is Confronting Beijing and Increasing Defense Ties with ASEAN Members to Protect Maritime Trade," *Wall Street Journal*, July 9, 2012, http://www.wsj.com/articles/SB10001424052702303567704577516252626896574.

44. Kato, "China's Naval Expansion in the Western Pacific," 19.

45. National Institute for Defense Studies, *NIDS China Security Report 2011*, 26.

46. Michèle Flournoy and Janine Davidson, "Obama's New Global Posture: The Logic of U.S. Foreign Deployments," *Foreign Affairs* 91, no. 4 (July/August 2012): 59.

47. Robert Ross, "The Problem of the Asia Pivot," *Foreign Affairs* 91, no. 6 (November/December 2012): 79.

power structure in East Asia.[48] Thus, Japan can strategically confront China's assertiveness in the South China Sea and assume an active role in the U.S.-Japan security alliance.

The Emergence of an East Asia Strategic Balance

China claims almost 80 percent of the South China Sea. However, it cannot exercise complete territorial control over the Spratlys and its surrounding waters because these land features are occupied by other claimant states, and, more significantly, because of the growing involvement of the United States and Japan in the maritime dispute. The United States is troubled by China's bullying behavior toward the small claimant states. By all appearances, it assumes that any Chinese use of force against Vietnam and the Philippines, a U.S. treaty ally, is a direct challenge to U.S. military supremacy and diplomatic influence in East Asia.

Meanwhile, Japan, concerned about how the Senkaku Islands dispute may play out, has become involved in the South China Sea dispute as well. The stable but fragile security situation can be described as a classic strategic balancing by two small powers that depend on other external major powers to maintain a precarious status quo in the South China Sea, both at present and for the foreseeable future.[49] On the dynamics of this balance of power system in Southeast Asia, as the Australia-based Lowy Institute for International Policy notes:

> The system assumes competition between states and hence the ever-present risk of aggression and conflict . . . in which participants agree, if only tacitly to curb competition for influence in the interest of maintaining system-wide stability.[50]

Key to the system is its inherent dynamism. If the power of one state grows disproportionately, the system adjusts through a realignment of the relationship among the others. Some states—those most susceptible to the gravitational pull of the growing power—will be attracted closer to it. Others will respond by drawing closer to each other and to an alternative pole or poles in the system. Some states will attempt a mix of both, as is evident in Southeast Asia.

The choice states make in response to a balance of power dynamic need not be based solely on power considerations. Questions of how benign they perceive a powerful state also influences their decisions about balancing or bandwagoning.[51]

Thus far, this balance of power system in the South China Sea has averted an armed conflict among claimant states, prompting Professor David Scott to quip that "the benefits

---

48. International Institute for Strategic Studies, *The Military Balance 2012: The Annual Assessment of Global Military Capabilities and Defence Economics* (London: International Institute for Strategic Studies, 2012), 212.
49. Scott, "Conflict Irresolution in the South China Sea," 1041.
50. Cook et al., *Power and Choice*, 25–26.
51. Ibid.

of such balancing may become apparent because balancing is itself a stabilizing process."[52] However, this situation has two major flaws. One is that it generates a very fluid situation wherein any error or miscalculation by any claimant state may trigger an armed confrontation, which may escalate or drag other maritime powers into a major systemic conflict. Second, while the balance-of-power system has stabilized the situation, it also simply failed to resolve the dispute, creating a tense and protracted impasse. The claimant states are using this lull to build up their respective military capabilities for any eventuality.

As a case in point, China has intentionally delayed the resolution of the dispute to fortify its control of the contested areas and dissuade other states from pursuing their claims.[53] This rules out any possibility of compromises. As a countermeasure, the Philippines and Vietnam have adopted a balancing strategy that draws the United States and Japan into the fray. These external maritime powers are just as anxious to curtail China's growing strategic clout in East Asia. At present, China finds itself trapped in its own security dilemma as it faces increasing U.S. and Japanese naval presence and pressure in the South China Sea. Despite decades of restructuring and modernization, Chinese leadership is not yet entirely confident that its untried (and inexperienced) armed forces can win wars under high-technology conditions when confronted by the U.S. Navy, supported by Japan's MSDF.[54] The International Institute for Strategic Studies observes that despite the PLA's ambition for a blue-water navy, China has yet to put in place all the assets necessary to form an effective carrier task group for blue-water capability.[55] If the balance of power works against its interests, however, China might use force on any of the claimant states that have cemented their security ties with the United States and Japan. Nonetheless, such maneuvering by China will surely invite possible intervention by these two maritime powers, especially if Chinese forces are seen as making a strategic push against U.S. (and Japanese) naval presence in the first island chain. In effect, the current balance-of-power system can become the proverbial calm before the storm.

China's use of force against any of the small claimant states can trigger this storm. For example, China's armed, hostile actions against the Philippines, a U.S. treaty ally, might push the United States to make adjustments, however difficult, to its policies in situations in which its less-than-vital interests are at stake. Such actions can also push the United States to accentuate the strategic risk posed by China's ever growing power and military capabilities.[56] On the one hand, failing to respond to China's use of force against its treaty ally will undermine the credibility of Washington's security guarantees to its Asian allies. Unless the United States backs its security guarantee with the use of force, its regional allies may grow fearful of being abandoned, lose the will to challenge China, and eventually succumb to appeasement. On the other hand, anticipating an expected U.S. intervention, Chinese

52. Scott, "Conflict Irresolution in the South China Sea," 1042.
53. Fravel, "China's Strategy in the South China Sea," 12.
54. Ren and Liu, "Transitional Security Pattern in the South China Sea and the Involvement of External Parties," 7.
55. International Institute for Strategic Studies, *The Military Balance 2012*, 213.
56. Charles Glaser, "Will China's Rise Lead to War? Why Realism Does not Mean Pessimism," *Foreign Affairs* 90, no. 2 (March/April 2011): 91.

strategic planners may be tempted to test their growing A2/AD capabilities to prevent the U.S. Navy from triggering a naval confrontation in the region. Worse, Chinese military leaders might convince themselves that if the United States is to intervene, the PLA could cripple U.S. conventional naval forces in the Western Pacific. On the possibility of a direct armed confrontation between China and the United States (and its allies), a U.S. academic warns:

> Should Beijing and Washington find themselves in a conflict, the huge U.S. advantage in conventional forces would increase the temptation for Washington to threaten to or actually use force. Recognizing the temptation facing Washington, Beijing might in turn feel pressure to use its conventional forces before they are destroyed. Although China could not reverse the military imbalance, it might believe that quickly imposing high costs on the United States would be the best way to get it to back off. . . . Under such circumstances, both Beijing and Washington would have incentives to initiate an attack.[57]

Balancing China's Maritime Expansion

The Philippines is a maritime and archipelagic state made of 7,107 islands and occupies a wide maritime area stretching 1,150 miles from about the 5th to the 20th parallels north latitude. Topographically, the country is fragmented by inland waters, which also gives the Philippines one of the longest coastlines of any country in the world. Aside from the ruggedness of the land mass, the Philippines has an irregular coastline that extends to about 10,850 miles, twice as long as that of the continental United States. It is also geographically isolated from mainland East Asia, as its maritime borders provide the country an almost impenetrable moat against any external threat emanating from the Asian mainland.

Thus, maritime security is vital for the Philippines as archipelagic state in Southeast Asia.[58] Historically however, the Philippines primarily focused its strategic attention and efforts on containing domestic insurgencies generated by economic inequality and the lack of national cohesion. Since 1946 Philippine national security concerns have been rooted in conflicts and the identity of the Philippine nation-state, especially over regime legitimacy, social justice, and socioeconomic inequality, which continue to create tension between state and society.[59] This resulted in the primacy of land-based security threats, and subordinated maritime security to internal security concerns and counterinsurgency operations. This condition was reinforced by the absence of any visible external threats emanating from the Philippines' maritime domain and the reliance on the United States for the country's external defense requirements.[60] This changed in the first decade of the twenty-first

57. Avery Goldstein, "China's Real and Present Danger: Now is the Time for Washington to Worry," *Foreign Affairs* 95, no. 5 (September/October 2013): 138–139.
58. Ronnie Gil L. Gavan, "Organized National Engagement (ONE) at Sea: Optimizing the State's Option for Maritime Security," *Digest* 19, no. 1 (2012): 1.
59. Noel M. Morada and Christopher Collier, "The Philippines: State versus Society," in *Asian Security Practice: Material and Ideational Influences*, ed. Muthiah Alagappa (Stanford, CA: Stanford University Press, 2001), 550.
60. Gavan, "Organized National Engagement (ONE) at Sea," 10.

century with China's emergence as a naval power in East Asia, and the election of President Benigno Aquino in May 2010.

On March 2, 2011, two Chinese patrol boats harassed a survey ship commissioned by the Philippine Department of Energy (DOE) to conduct oil exploration in the Reed Bank (now called Recto Bank in the Philippines). The Reed Bank lies about 95 miles east of the Spratly Islands and 150 miles west of the Philippine island of Palawan. Stunned by this maritime encounter, which happened within the Philippines' EEZ, the Aquino administration filed a protest with the Chinese embassy in Manila. A Department of Foreign Affairs spokesperson said that the Philippines was simply seeking an explanation for the incident.[61] Brushing aside the Philippines' complaint, a Chinese embassy official insisted that China has indisputable sovereignty over the Spratly Islands and their adjacent territory. Beijing then went on to demand that Manila first seek Chinese permission before it could conduct oil exploration activities even within the Philippines' EEZ. Furthermore, China badgered the Philippines and other claimant states into recognizing China's sovereign claim over the South China Sea.[62] Its heavy-handed attitude and arrogant pronouncements against the Philippines and Vietnam in the first half of 2011 escalated the territorial dispute. By then, Aquino unmistakably saw that the Philippines is on a direct collision course with China vis-à-vis the South China Sea issue.

With these incidents, the Aquino administration hastened to develop territorial defense capabilities of the Armed Forces of the Philippines (AFP). In June 2011 the executive branch of the Philippine government and the AFP agreed on a multiyear, multibillion peso defense upgrade spending and military buildup. In October 2011 Defense Secretary Voltaire Gazmin released a defense planning guidance for the 2013–2018 period, which aims to restructure the AFP into a lean but fully capable armed forces to confront the challenges to the country's territorial integrity and maritime security.

The Philippines' immediate territorial defense goal is to establish a modest but "comprehensive border protection program" anchored on the surveillance, deterrence, and border patrol capabilities of the Philippine air force, navy, and coast guard.[63] This monitoring and modest force projection capability stretches the country's territorial waters to its contiguous zone and EEZ. The long-term goal, according to the 2011 *Armed Forces of the Philippines: Strategic Intent*, is to develop the force structure and capabilities crucial to maintain a "credible deterrent posture against foreign intrusion or external aggression, and other illegal activities while allowing free navigation to prosper."[64] The most recent defense planning guidance states, "That the defense of the country's territorial integrity

61. Norman Bordadora, "Philippines Protests Chinese Harassment," *Philippine Daily Inquirer*, April 3, 2011, http://globalnation.inquirer.net/viewpoints/viewpoints/view/20110304-323451/PH-protests-Chinese-harassment.

62. "China Wants Philippines to Seek Permission before Spratlys Oil Search," BBC Monitoring Asia-Pacific, June 10, 2011.

63. National Security Council, *National Security Policy 2011–2016* (Quezon City: National Security Council, 2011), 39.

64. Office of the Deputy Chief of Staff, *Armed Forces of the Philippines: Strategic Intent* (Quezon City: Camp Aguinaldo, 2011), 27.

and sovereignty, specifically in the West Philippine Sea, poses [as] the most foremost security challenge. . . . Hence, the primary end goal of the department is to develop a minimum credible posture for territorial defense and maritime security."[65]

This requires the AFP to develop an effective force present in the area that exhibits the competence to defend the territory, and greater surveillance and monitoring to further secure the Philippine islands and prevent unoccupied islands/reefs from being occupied by other claimants.[66]

Building Up a Credible Defense Posture

Although determined to shift the AFP's focus from internal security to territorial defense, the Aquino administration is constrained by insufficient financial resources even for its modest defense acquisition goals. The current territorial defense buildup is a very expensive undertaking because, in many cases, the AFP has to start from scratch. For example, the Philippine air defense capability is nil because the Philippine air force is practically a helicopter air force without any fighter planes. It has only one operational radar with a very limited coverage area.[67] The air force needs to develop or acquire radars, hangars, forward operating bases, maintenance, as well as command and control facilities. The Philippine navy plans to acquire two state-of-the-art frigates, which could be equipped with communications and weapons systems and mission essential devices such as day/night electronic navigational gadgets, communication suites, safety-of-life-at-sea equipment, propulsion and seamanship and ship-handling gears, and corresponding logistic support packages.

The financial constraints on the Aquino administration's modernization programs are apparent in its efforts to acquire big-ticket items for the air force and navy. In November 2011 Aquino announced the air force's projected purchase of two squadrons of second-hand F-16C/D through the U.S. excess defense articles.[68] This acquisition, however, might cause tremendous financial strains on the AFP, which is still actively engaged in internal security operations. In fact, as part of the AFP's Oplan Bayanihan (Operational Plan Community Spirit), the air force continues to carry out counterinsurgency/counterterrorism functions, including intelligence, surveillance, and reconnaissance; precision attacks to minimize collateral damages for the army's ground support operations; and education and information dissemination campaigns to win the people's hearts and minds.

---

65. Secretary of the Department of Defense, *Defense: Planning Guidance 2016–2017* (Quezon City: Department of Defense, March 2015), 4.
66. Ibid.
67. For an interesting discussion on the dismal state of the Philippine air force, see Galileo Gerard R. Kintanar, "Developing an Air Power Culture—the Missing Dimension," *Digest: Strategic and Special Studies* (Third Quarter 2012): 35–48.
68. Jon Grevatt, "Philippines to Hasten Recreation of Dedicated Combat Wing with Ex-USAF F-16 Purchase," *IHS Jane's Defense Industry* 29, no. 1 (2012).

In May 2012 Aquino hinted that the air force might acquire brand-new lead-in jet trainers that could be converted into fighter planes.[69] In an interview, he admitted that the government found these too expensive to buy and maintain. A sound alternative, he said, is to buy cheaper new fighter aircraft from the United Kingdom, France, Italy, or South Korea.

In October 2012 the Philippine government started negotiations for the procurement of 12 Korean F/A-50 Golden Eagles from the Korean Aerospace Industries (KAI). The F/A-50's design was largely patterned after the U.S.-built Lockheed Martin F-16 Fighting Falcons. Both models have similar features: single engine, and the same speed, size, cost, and range of weapon systems. These 12 F/A-50 interceptors can secure the Philippines' airspace and simultaneously serve as trainer planes to develop air force pilots' air command maneuvering skills.[70] During his two-day visit to South Korea in October 2013, Aquino announced that the two governments were in the process of finalizing the deal, which was estimated to be worth $450 million (18.9 billion pesos).

In March 2014, after nearly two years of difficult and tedious negotiations, the Philippines finally signed a contract with KAI for the purchase of fighter planes. Guaranteed by the state-owned Korea Trade-Investment Promotion Agency, the contract commits KAI to deliver the fighter planes to the Philippine air force within the next 38 months. With air-to-air mid-distance attack and night-fighting capabilities, the 12 F/A-50s will act as interim jet fighters until the Philippine air force has more funding and the training needed to purchase fourth-generation multirole combat interceptors.[71] This has long been the air force's plans since the Philippines bought 25 F-8 Crusader fighter-bombers from the United States in 1979 to supplement its squadrons of pre-Vietnam War F-5 fighter planes. Thus the acquisition of F/A-50 fighter planes was an important milestone for the Philippine air force, which has had no operational fighter planes since the retirement of its two aging squadrons of Northrop F-5s in 2005. This was also the AFP's first big-ticket acquisition since it began its force modernization in the early 1990s.

The Aquino administration has also funded the Philippine navy's desired force mix, an acquisition program aimed to give it limited anti-air/anti-submarine capabilities. Since 2012 the navy has been pushing for the acquisition of two frigates for territorial defense, internal security operations, naval interdiction, and humanitarian assistance and disaster response. These vessels will be equipped with air-to-air, anti-ship and anti-submarine weapons and sensors for extended and extensive patrolling and surveillance of the country's vast maritime territory. Initially, the Department of National Defense was mulling over buying two decommissioned Italian *Maestrale*-class frigates, which have credible

69. Aurea Calica, "Aquino: Government Can Now Afford to Buy New Fighter Jets," *Philippine Star*, May 17, 2012, http://www.philstar.com/headlines/807430/aquino-government-can-now-afford-buy-new-fighter-jets.

70. "Philippines: F/A-50s to Boost Country's Capability to Defend Territory," Asia News Monitor, October 21, 2013.

71. "South Korea, Philippines Sign Agreement on Export of Fighter Aircraft," BBC Monitoring Asia-Pacific, March 28, 2014.

missile and anti-submarine capabilities. However, the department eventually decided against the purchase after evaluation studies found that operating these second-hand vessels would be costlier in the long run.[72]

The government has looked at offers made by South Korea and Spain to supply two brand-new frigates for the Philippine navy. However the project has been on hold for the past two years because the navy is in a quandary over whether it should acquire cheaper, second-hand ships or more expensive, newly constructed vessels. In the end, however, the final decision will likely depend on whether there is an exigent need for the frigates and, more essentially, the availability of public funds for the acquisition of these ships. As one ranking defense official notes, only vessels that will provide the country a "credible defense posture" and (more importantly) affordable cost will be selected.[73]

In addition to its frigate requirements, the Philippine navy needs to replace its fleet of World War II–era surface combatants with new vessels. In 2011 the Philippine government could only acquire two former U.S. Coast Guard cutters for the navy. Since the deployment of modern frigates requires increased endurance support for long-term maritime operations, the navy will also need at-sea replenishment and fueling capabilities in the next five years. The navy also needs to build bigger piers for its larger vessels and new maritime surveillance radar systems for its new naval facilities.[74] Finally the Philippine navy has to train its officers and sailors to man and equip new, modern ships. Furthermore, the acquisition of new ships from different sources means that naval officers and crews must continuously learn different systems and shiphandling characteristics.

Besides efforts to build up the Philippines' territorial defense capabilities, the Aquino administration has ardently challenged China's expansive claims in the South China Sea and its encroachments into the Philippines' EEZ. However, bogged down by insufficient resources, the AFP's modernization process could hardly deter the PLAN in the South China Sea given the latter's procurement of large surface combatants and submarines since the advent of the twenty-first century.[75] Even if the Philippine government provides the AFP the funds it needs to shop for planes, surface combatants, and submarines, the strategic imbalance between the Philippines and China cannot be rectified in the foreseeable future. Fortunately for the country, two external powers, the United States and Japan, are interested in fostering a security partnership with the Philippines in the face of China's maritime expansion in the South China Sea.

---

72. "Philippines: DND Eyes Acquisition of Two Brand New Frigates," Asia News Monitor, August 15, 2013.

73. "Only Best, Affordable Naval Ships Will Be Acquired for the Philippines," Asia News Monitor, January 9, 2013.

74. Rahmat Ridzwan, "Philippine Plans to Upgrade Naval Bases Hit by Lack of Funds," *IHS Jane's Navy International* 119, no. 6 (2014).

75. Richard A. Bitzinger, "Recent Developments in Naval and Maritime Modernization in the Asia-Pacific: Implication for Regional Security," in *The Chinese Navy: Expanding Capabilities, Evolving Roles*, ed. Phillip C. Saunders, Christopher Yung, Michael Swaine, and Andrew Nien-Dzu Yang (Washington, DC: National Defense University, 2011), 24.

Facilitating the U.S. Strategic Rebalancing to Asia

An important component in the Aquino administration's balancing policy with regard to China is the reconfigured Philippine-U.S. security relationship. The United States regularly extends technical and military assistance to the AFP under the auspices of the Philippine-U.S. treaty alliance. The most recent U.S. assistance included the transfer of two former U.S. Coast Guard's *Hamilton*-class cutters to the Philippine navy through the foreign military sales program.[76] Aware of its military inadequacies, however, Manila has asked for an unequivocal U.S. commitment to Philippine defense and security as provided for in the 1951 Mutual Defense Treaty, specifically U.S. naval and air support for Philippine forces in the Spratly Islands.

Philippine officials often rationalize that an armed attack on Philippine metropolitan territory and forces anywhere in the Pacific, including the South China Sea, should trigger an automatic U.S. armed response. The U.S. position on this matter, however, has been ambiguous for two reasons.[77] On the one hand, the United States has sought to address legitimate Philippine concerns about the absence of a clear guarantee of military support in case of an armed confrontation in the South China Sea. On the other hand, the United States has avoided giving an explicit or broad statement of a security guarantee, which it fears might encourage the Philippines to behave provocatively against China based on Manila's expansive interpretation of its sovereignty over islands it controls in the South China Sea, as well as a mistaken assumption about the prospect of an automatic U.S. armed response in case of an outbreak of hostility in the disputed waters.

Yet an increasing number of U.S. analysts have begun to share the view that the Philippines is a strategic bellwether of China's maritime expansion in the Western Pacific and at the same time a natural barrier to check China's expansionism.[78] Hence the United States should help the Philippines develop its own naval capabilities to counter China's efforts at power projection in the Asia Pacific.[79] In August 2011 Manila and Washington formulated a framework for heightened bilateral and multilateral security and domain awareness. The new framework considered the following five measures:

1. Rotational presence of U.S. maritime defense assets in the Philippines while the AFP develops its territorial defense capabilities.

2. Increased joint bilateral maritime security activities in the South China Sea.

3. Development of joint-use maritime security support facilities.

76. "Philippine Navy to Acquire Largest Ship in Inventory," GMA News, January 23, 2011.

77. See Sheena Chestnut Greitens, "The U.S. Alliance with the Philippines: Challenges and Opportunities," in *Strategic Asia 2014–15: U.S. Alliances and Partnership at the Center of Global Power*, ed. Ashley J. Tellis, Abraham M. Denmark, and Greg Chaffin (Seattle: National Bureau of Asian Research, 2014), 144.

78. Ibid., 128.

79. Ibid.

4. Improved information sharing between U.S. and Philippine forces.
5. Conducting integrated maritime security initiatives between the U.S. Pacific Command and the AFP.[80]

These initiatives aim to compensate for the AFP's limited territorial defense capabilities, and expedite joint operations in case the Mutual Defense Treaty is invoked because of a potential armed attack against the Philippines.[81]

The 2012 Scarborough Shoal standoff and later China's occupation of the shoal made it urgent for Manila to negotiate a framework agreement on increased rotational presence, which evolved into the Enhanced Defense Cooperation Agreement (EDCA), with Washington. The agreement would facilitate the deployment of U.S. troops and equipment to the Philippines on a rotational basis, thus skirting the controversial issue of reestablishing U.S. bases in the country. Furthermore, with its small and weak naval force and an almost nonexistent air force, the Philippine military will benefit from greater U.S. technical assistance in joint military training, humanitarian missions, and disaster response operations.

On August 14, 2013, negotiations on the defense agreement started in Manila. The Pentagon had earlier clarified that it is not establishing permanent bases reminiscent of the Cold War, but only wants to maintain a strategic footprint in Southeast Asia.[82] This policy statement reassured Manila that Washington has neither the desire nor the interest to create U.S. bases in Southeast Asia.[83] After five rounds of negotiations, the two sides produced a working draft that incorporated and observed areas that the Philippines might regard as constitutional red lines.[84] By March 31, 2014, an agreement on expanded U.S. rotational deployment in Southeast Asia was finalized. A few weeks later Evan Medeiros, U.S. National Security Council director for Asian affairs, announced that forces would have temporary access to and be able to preposition fighter jets and ships at selected Philippine military bases.[85] He described the agreement as "the most significant defense agreement that the United States has concluded with the Philippines in decades."[86]

On April 28, 2014, Philippine defense secretary Gazmin and U.S. ambassador to the Philippines Philip Goldberg signed what became known as the EDCA a few hours before

---

80. Philippine-U.S. Mutual Defense Board/Security Engagement Board Co-Chairmen, "2011 Mutual Defense/Board Engagement Board Strategic Guidelines," August 16, 2011.

81. Greg Torode, "U.S. Under Pressure over Sea Dispute," *South China Morning Post*, June 17, 2011, http://www.scmp.com/article/970856/us-under-pressure-over-sea-dispute.

82. Craig Whitlock, "Philippines May Allow Greater U.S. Military Presence in Reaction to China's Rise," *Washington Post*, January 26, 2012, https://www.washingtonpost.com/world/national-security/philippines-may-allow-greater-us-presence-in-latest-reaction-to-chinas-rise/2012/01/24/gIQAhFIyQQ_story.html.

83. Ibid.

84. Ibid.

85. Jim Gomez, "US, Philippines Reach Deal on Troops," Associated Press, April 28, 2014, http://news.yahoo.com/apnewsbreak-us-philippines-reach-deal-troops-061639123.html.

86. Juliet Eilperin, "U.S., Philippines Reach 10-Year Defense Agreement Amid Rising Tension," *Washington Post*, April 27, 2014, https://www.washingtonpost.com/world/us-philippines-to-sign-10-year-defense-agreement-amid-rising-tensions/2014/04/27/a04436c0-cddf-11e3-a75e-463587891b57_story.html.

President Barack Obama arrived in Manila for his first official visit. The EDCA is not a new security pact, it is merely an updated version of the 1951 Mutual Defense Treaty.[87] This executive agreement provides the framework by which the Philippines and the United States can develop their individual and collective defense capabilities. Although the EDCA allows American forces to utilize facilities owned and controlled by the AFP, the Philippine base commander has unhampered access to the facility. Likewise, the AFP will be able to use the infrastructure that the U.S. military builds or improves at these facilities. Furthermore, any construction and activities within Philippine bases will require the consent of the host country. However, the EDCA is currently awaiting a ruling by the Philippine Supreme Court over its constitutionality and whether it will need senate ratification.

On a strategic level, the EDCA, if carried out, would undercut China's A2/AD strategy in Southeast Asia, without the United States establishing any permanent bases in the region. Since the late 1990s, the PLA has been developing strategies and acquiring weapon systems that could disrupt U.S. naval and air operations in the Western Pacific, or slow down the deployment of U.S. air and naval forces to the theater of operations.[88] The Chinese military could, in the long run, even prevent U.S. forces from operating in certain locations, or force U.S. naval ships and planes to operate from distances farther than the U.S. military would otherwise prefer.[89]

Through the EDCA, however, U.S. forces are afforded two innovative access arrangements in the Philippines. They are forward operating sites (expandable warm military facilities with limited U.S. military support presence) and cooperative security locations (facilities with little or no permanent American presence that are maintained by the host country).[90] This system allows the United States to bring U.S. tactical units, including personnel and equipment, to allied bases in East Asia for planning purposes or to carry out contingency missions in a crisis or conflict situation.[91] These access arrangements are less expensive, less visible, and less vulnerable, while offering U.S. forces greater strategic and operational flexibility. They are also less likely to create local problems—as permanent bases would—and are expected to promote sustainable security cooperation between the United States and the Philippines. By relying on "places not bases," the U.S. Pacific Command can expand its area of operations and responsibility. More significantly, if EDCA can be implemented, U.S. access to operationally flexible facilities under the agreement, which would be located all over a sprawling archipelagic country located near China, can derail the PLA's A2/AD strategy. Also, U.S. naval and air assets in these temporary air and naval sites will help expedite the rapid and massive deployment of U.S. forces if hostilities break out in the South China Sea, or even in the East China Sea.

---

87. "New Defense Agreement Enhances Philippine, U.S. Alliance on Security Challenges—DND Chief," Philippines News Agency, April 28, 2014.

88. Cliff et al., *Entering the Dragon's Lair*, xvii.

89. Ibid.

90. For details regarding this new form of access arrangements, see Robert Harkavy, "Thinking about Basing," *Naval War College Review* 58, no. 3 (2005): 12–42.

91. Ibid., 1.

Fostering a Strategic Partnership with Japan

In addition to strengthening its alliance with the United States, the Philippines has also fostered its ties with Japan, China's main rival in East Asia. In 2011 Tokyo and Manila upgraded bilateral ties between Japan and the Philippines to a strategic partnership. After Aquino's third visit to Japan in 2011 Tokyo and Manila held high-level talks on maritime affairs and exchanges between Philippine and Japanese defense and maritime officials. The two sides also agreed that Japan would provide capacity-building training for the 3,500-strong Philippine coast guard.[92] In September 2011 Aquino and new Japanese prime minister Yoshihiko Noda issued a joint statement in Tokyo, affirming that the South China Sea is vital as "it connects the world and the Asia Pacific, and that peace and stability therein is of common interest to the international community."[93] Kan also instructed the Japanese coast guard to further train the Philippine coast guard, consult regularly with Philippine naval officers, and increase joint coast guard exercises.[94]

In July 2012 Gazmin and Japanese defense minister Satoshi Morimoto inked a bilateral agreement on maritime security.[95] This agreement features high-level dialogues between high-ranking defense officials and reciprocal visits by the MSDF's chief of staff and the Philippine navy's flag commander. A few days later Philippine foreign affairs secretary Albert Del Rosario announced that Tokyo was likely to provide the Philippine coast guard with 10 40-meter boats as part of Japan's official development assistance to the Philippines by the end of the year.[96] Newspapers also reported a grant of two additional bigger vessels that were considered for transfer to the Philippine government.

In January 2013 Japanese foreign minister Fumio Kishida announced Japan's technical assistance to the Philippine coast guard through the provision of essential communications systems equipment for maritime safety.[97] In June 2013 Gazmin and Japanese defense minister Itsunori Onodera confirmed the continuous "exchanges of information aimed at strengthening Philippine-Japan defense relations and on working together to make the U.S. strategic rebalancing a reality in Asia."[98] Gazmin also raised the possibility of allowing the MSDF access to former U.S. military bases in the Philippines if Tokyo is interested in signing an access agreement with Manila.[99]

---

92. "Japan and Philippines Strengthen Maritime Security Ties," *Jane's Country Risk Daily Report* 18, no. 195 (2011).
93. Christian V. Esguerra, "Philippines Gets Japan Support on Spratlys Dispute," *Philippine Daily Inquirer*, September 28, 2011, http://globalnation.inquirer.net/13915/philippines-gets-japan-support-on-spratlys-dispute.
94. James Hookway and Yoree Koh, "Japan, Philippines Seek Tighter Ties to Counter China," *Wall Street Journal*, September 27, 2011, http://www.wsj.com/articles/SB10001424052970204422404576594521640016158.
95. "Japan and Philippines Sign Defense Pact," *Jane's Country Risk Daily Report* 19, no. 134 (2012).
96. Jerry E. Esplanada, "Philippines, Japan to Enhance Maritime Security Ties," *Philippine Daily Inquirer*, July 9, 2012, http://globalnation.inquirer.net/43508/philippines-japan-to-enhance-maritime-security-ties.
97. "Philippines, Japan Agree to Enhance Cooperation in Maritime Security," Asia News Monitor, January 14, 2013.
98. "Philippines, Japan Agree to Strengthen Defense Ties," BBC Monitoring Asia-Pacific, June 27, 2013.
99. Ibid.

The Philippines and Japan have conducted high-level meetings and consultations to solidify their security cooperation in the face of China's military assertiveness. In December 2013 Aquino and Prime Minister Shinzo Abe in Tokyo discussed their concerns about China's establishment of an air defense identification zone (ADIZ) in the East China Sea.[100] Aquino was worried that China might extend the zone into the South China Sea, adversely affecting Philippine security. Abe assured Aquino that Japan would not tolerate China's attempt to change the status quo in the region by force, and reaffirmed his intentions to cooperate with the Philippines to ensure that the freedom of overflight and navigation is respected.[101] To help build up the Philippine coast guard's capability, Abe approved a soft loan worth approximately $184 million to finance the Philippines' acquisition of 10 130-foot long multipurpose patrol boats from Japan.

In June 2014 Aquino and Abe met again in Tokyo to discuss ways to further Philippine-Japan security relations.[102] Aquino followed up on the Philippine coast guard's request to acquire the 10 aforementioned patrol boats. Abe assured Aquino that three of the vessels would be delivered in 2015, while the remaining seven will be ready for delivery in 2016.

The Philippine coast guard needs more patrol boats to secure the waters around the seven islands claimed and occupied by the Philippines in the Spratlys. These boats will also monitor foreign naval presence in the several reefs and shoals within the Philippines' EEZ currently occupied by Chinese forces. To assist the Philippine coast guard's maritime domain awareness operations, Japan promised to provide very small aperture terminal, or VSAT, and Inmarsat communication systems.

More significantly, Aquino has strongly endorsed Abe's plans to expand Japan's security role in the region. In light of the Sino-Japanese dispute over the Senkaku Islands, Abe has pushed for the reinterpretation of the pacifist 1947 Japanese constitution to enable the SDF to assist allies such as the United States in case of a conflict, even if Japan is not attacked. Aquino boldly declared that expanding the MSDF's role and cementing bilateral economic and security ties between the Philippines and Japan would help ensure regional security.[103]

In his recent visit to Japan in early June 2015, Aquino and Abe signed a joint declaration on strengthening the Philippine-Japan strategic partnership. The communiqué commits Japan to enhancing the capacity of the Philippine coast guard, cooperating with the Philippines on maritime security and specifically on maritime domain awareness, and transferring Japanese defense equipment and technology to the Philippines.[104] In a press briefing, Aquino announced forthcoming negotiations on a status of forces agreement that would

100. "Japan, Philippines to Cooperate on China's Air Defense Zone," Jiji Press, December 13, 2013.
101. Ibid.
102. "Aquino and Abe Discuss Maritime Disputes," *Gulf News*, June 25, 2014.
103. Alexander Martin, "Philippine President Backs Abe's Military Push," *Wall Street Journal*, June 24, 2014, http://www.wsj.com/articles/philippine-president-backs-abes-military-push-1403594118.
104. Ministry of Foreign Affairs of Japan, "Japan-Philippines Joint Declaration: A Strengthened Partnership for Advancing the Shared Principles and Goals of Peace, Security, and Growth in the Region and Beyond," accessed August 26, 2015, http://www.mofa.go.jp/files/000083585.pdf.

allow the SDF access to Philippine military bases. He said that such an agreement is possible because the two countries have boosted their security relations significantly over the past few years. The SDF's use of Philippine bases on a limited and rotational basis will be useful as Japan actively pursues a greater security role in the Asia-Pacific region. With refueling and basing facilities in the Philippines, the air and maritime units of the SDF can also conduct joint patrols with their U.S. counterparts for a longer period of time and over a larger area of the South China Sea.

Conclusion

The Philippines has taken advantage of what appears to be strategic impasse among the major powers—the United States, China, and Japan—as it builds up a credible defense capability to back its defiant act of standing up to China's maritime expansion in the South China Sea. It has also strengthened its security ties with the United States and Japan to maintain the balance of power in the region for the time being. However, given the slow pace of and the limited funding for its arms modernization programs, the Philippines foresees that this strategic standoff among the major powers will continue way into the third decade of the twenty-first century. This strategic standoff may just be the proverbial calm before the storm. If this storm suddenly breaks out on its maritime horizons, the Philippines might find itself in the same situation as it was in late 1941—militarily ill-equipped, utterly defenseless, and totally unprepared for the tempest's destructive onslaught.

2 | The Military Balance and Regional Order in the South China Sea

Patrick M. Cronin

We have entered a period of intensified competition in the South China Sea. Maritime tensions in Asia are growing and will persist, and yet relations are likely to remain bounded below the threshold of military conflict. All sides are positioning themselves to gain the upper hand and to minimize less advantageous positions. While we can still expect tactical maneuvering before and after summit meetings, strategic dialogues, and regional conferences, we should not expect tensions to completely subside even when cooperation is the official position. Notwithstanding calls for grand bargains and strategic accommodation, we will be navigating in the messy middle ground between war and peace well into the next U.S. administration. Although such volatility will be uncomfortable, achieving a firmer footing with China will likewise be difficult.

Despite a kind of racetrack mentality in the press, this maneuvering for advantage and to determine the rule set governing regional order is not primarily a question of comparing military orders of battle. Consequently, analysts should refrain from a disquisition on bean counting in the South China Sea. After all, to do so would exaggerate the extent to which military modernization and the gradual buildup and deployment of arms and military platforms will determine the stability of this vital maritime region. In addition, a narrow discussion comparing military orders of battle would miss the most important political dimensions of strategic competition under way in and around the South China Sea.

The paper will instead focus on the primary competition, which has more to do with a reemerging China's capacity and desire for expanding its influence over its neighbors and adjacent waters, en route to securing a position as *a* if not *the* major global power in the twenty-first century.

The Rising Importance of Asia and the South China Sea

The driving force behind the United States' gradual rebalance to the Indo-Pacific region is rooted in long-term trend lines. For the first time since the eighteenth century, Asia is becoming the locus of the global economy and world politics. Based on its combined gross domestic product (GDP), population levels, defense spending, and investments in technology, Asia is projected to overtake both North America and Europe in terms of global power by 2030. China has been the largest growth engine, but a more comprehensive analysis shows that most of Asia has grown, is growing, and will keep rising.[1]

Asia has grown by an impressive order of magnitude. From the opening of China to the end of this decade, the GDP of Asia will have expanded some tenfold, and the growth of the Association of Southeast Asian Nations (ASEAN) as a percentage of global GDP may have doubled. Asia is growing faster than any other region around the globe. According to a 2015 study by the International Monetary Fund, the Asia-Pacific region will realize about 5.6 percent growth, roughly the same as last year and roughly the projected estimate for next year. Sub-Saharan Africa is the only other region that has even come close to this rate of growth.[2]

According to PricewaterhouseCoopers, one of the world's leading accounting firms, the reawakening of China, India, and Southeast Asia countries will drive the global economy in coming decades. By midcentury, Indonesia is expected to move from the ninth to the fourth largest economy (achieving perhaps a $42 trillion economy), and the Philippines may be the 20th largest economy (achieving an estimated $3.5 trillion economy). Asia will also be home to most of the world's burgeoning middle classes, with Vietnam, for instance, expected to see a doubling of its middle class between 2014 and 2020.[3] Thus, while military power remains important, economic metrics remain more compelling in assessing the growing importance of Southeast Asia and the wider Indo-Pacific region.

Another important metric relates to demographics, although these statistics are affecting different Asian countries in different ways. The world is currently home to more than 7 billion people. The global population may surpass 8 billion by 2025 and perhaps 9 billion by 2050. Asia is home to six of the most populous countries in the world (including Indonesia). Southeast Asia's population is more than 633 million, and by 2020 about half of Southeast Asia's population will be under 30 years of age. Demographic trends will make Southeast Asia more influential, as its growing urban markets will likely be filled with more and better educated and better off middle classes.

It is not just money and people, but also goods being traded through the South China Sea that are important. Half of the world's commercial shipping by tonnage (worth more than $5.3 trillion) sails through the South China Sea. Some noted analysts, including Robert Kaplan, have argued that the South China Sea is to China what the Caribbean was to the

1. For instance, see Matthew Burrows, *The Future, Declassified: Megatrends That Will Undo the World Unless We Take Action* (New York: St. Martin's Press, 2014).

2. International Monetary Fund, *Regional Economic Outlook: Asia and Pacific: Stabilizing and Outperforming Other Regions* (Washington, DC: International Monetary Fund, 2015), http://www.imf.org/external/pubs/ft/reo/2015/apd/eng/pdf/areo0415.pdf.

3. See PricewaterhouseCoopers, *The World in 2050* (London: PricewaterhouseCoopers, February 2015), http://www.pwc.com/gx/en/issues/the-economy/assets/world-in-2050-february-2015.pdf.

United States,[4] but this analogy does not fully capture the true significance of the South China Sea because of three key differences.

First, the twenty-first century is or should be based on the rule of law, and not spheres of influence as in the nineteenth century. Second, the ASEAN economies (whose collective GDP is pushing $4 trillion in purchasing power parity) are much larger than those of the Caribbean. And third, the South China Sea is vital for the global economy in a way that the Caribbean was not (although admittedly it became more important for the United States after the Spanish-American War and for global trade after the building of the Panama Canal). But the South China Sea surpasses other historical examples as a major maritime passageway going forward. As the U.S. Department of Defense's 2015 *Asia-Pacific Maritime Security Strategy* states, "The importance of Asia-Pacific sea lanes for global trade cannot be overstated."[5] As proof of this claim, the strategy goes on to note that "almost 30 percent of the world's maritime trade transits the South China Sea annually . . . and in 2014, more than 15 million barrels of oil passed through the Malacca Strait per day."[6]

China's Assertiveness and Military Modernization Are Unsettling Stability

All these factors underlie the growing military importance of Asia, both in absolute and relative terms. Asians now spend more on defense than do Europeans, and Asian defense spending is rising at a time when global military spending has been in decline. The Stockholm International Peace Research Institute's 2015 annual report demonstrates that while overall global military spending is down slightly for a third year in a row, defense spending in the Asia Pacific has risen by 5 percent compared to 2014.[7] Regional military spending has reached a total $439 billion and rising, as China continues to set the pace with a 9.7 percent increase.[8] Other Asian countries worried about a growing regional military imbalance, especially in the South China Sea, will follow suit. Some already have; for instance, since 2005, Vietnam's defense spending has risen 128 percent.[9] These trends are likely to continue, with India recently announcing an 11 percent increase in defense spending for the year ahead, and Indonesia likely to trend upward after a recent temporary dip in spending.

China is inevitably the key driver behind these trends. The Center for a New American Security (CNAS) began tracking China's pattern of assertiveness in 2009.[10] Since then,

4. Robert Kaplan, *Asia's Cauldron: The South China Sea and the End of a Stable Pacific* (New York: Random House, 2014).
5. Department of Defense, *Asia-Pacific Maritime Security Strategy* (Washington, DC: Department of Defense, 2015), 1.
6. Ibid.
7. Sam Perlo-Freeman, Aude Fleurant, Pieter D. Wezeman, and Siemon T. Wezeman, "Trends in World Military Expenditure, 2014," SIPRI Fact Sheet, April 2015, http://books.sipri.org/files/FS/SIPRIFS1504.pdf.
8. Ibid.
9. Ibid.
10. See Patrick M. Cronin and Alexander Sullivan, *Preserving the Rules: Countering Coercion in Maritime Asia* (Washington, DC: Center for a New American Security, 2015); Ely Ratner, Elbridge Colby, Andrew Erickson, Zachary Hosford, and Alexander Sullivan, *More Willing and Able: Charting China's International Activism*

China has transitioned from a hide-and-bide approach to a far more active and assertive phase in and beyond the South China Sea. While China has become marginally more transparent, in important areas it is as opaque as ever. As with China's expansive nine-dash line claims to the South China Sea, there appear to be important areas of policy that China simply has not clarified.

In *Crouching Tiger: What China's Militarism Means for the World*, Peter Navarro systematically and concisely catalogues how China is shifting the regional military balance.[11] Key chapters, along with U.S. Department of Defense white papers and other recent studies and reports, highlight the following trends:

- The real (as opposed to official) budget of the People's Liberation Army (PLA) now surpasses $200 billion, yet China's near doubt-digit annual growth in defense spending is being achieved by spending about 2 percent of China's GDP versus the nearly 4 percent of GDP the United States has been spending on defense.[12] While it may take up to two more decades (according to one estimate[13]) for China's overall defense spending to surpass that of the United States, China enjoys vast strategic depth and land bases from which to achieve its goal of becoming a maritime power.
- China's military research and development builds defense platforms on a dual track: low-cost quantity (to flood the zone and good enough for taking on most neighbors) and high-end quality (to challenge U.S. power projection).[14]
- China is building many more cost-effective capabilities to deny and ultimately control sea and airspace, as well as cyber and outer space, in and around South China Sea and East China Sea; these are commonly referred to by U.S. defense officials as anti-access and area denial (A2/AD) capabilities.
- China is pursuing a positioning strategy through its incremental salami slicing in the South China Sea. Its island-building binge is not just to make its nine-dash line claim a de facto reality, thereby preempting international legal proceedings, but also to gain leverage over its neighbors and intimidate them into aligning with China.
- Consistent with China's non-kinetic three warfares (informational, legal, and psychological), this positioning is partly physical and partly psychological. Consider the

---

(Washington, DC: Center for a New American Security, 2015); Patrick M. Cronin, Ely Ratner, Elbridge Colby, Zachary M. Hosford, and Alexander Sullivan, *Tailored Coercion: Competition and Risk in Maritime Asia* (Washington, DC: Center for a New American Security, 2014); and Patrick M. Cronin, ed., *Cooperation from Strength: The United States, China and the South China Sea* (Washington, DC: Center for a New American Security, 2012). All are available and can be viewed or downloaded at www.cnas.org.

11. Peter Navarro, *Crouching Tiger: What China's Militarism Means for the World* (New York: Prometheus Books, 2015).

12. According to the SIPRI Fact Sheet, China's military budget in 2014 was an estimated $216 billion. See Perlo-Freeman et al., "Trends in World Military Expenditure, 2014."

13. See "China's Military Rise: The Dragon's New Teeth," *Economist*, April 7, 2012, http://www.economist.com/node/21552193.

14. See Tai Ming Cheung, "Conclusions," in *Forging China's Military Might: A New Framework for Assessing Innovation*, ed. Tai Ming Cheung (Baltimore, MD: Johns Hopkins University Press, 2014), 277.

recent accounts of Filipinos on Thitu (Pagasa) Island watching the lights of Chinese maritime engineers working to create facilities that could put at risk the marine resources of Reed Bank, Second Thomas (Ayungin) Shoal, and beyond.[15] One message China may want to send might be that Scarborough Shoal could be turned into a military facility like Fiery Cross Reef or Mischief Reef if the Philippines continues to challenge China or if there is a low-risk opportunity for China to proceed.

- China is slowly realizing Admiral Liu Huaqing's dream of sea control and a blue-water navy. As the father of the modern Chinese navy, Liu is the same military officer who authorized attacks on Vietnamese sailors so that China might occupy more of the Paracel Islands in 1974. Even more sobering, he commanded troops responsible for the Tiananmen Square massacre.[16] While Chinese aircraft carriers will make prime targets for adversaries, their deployment and development is significant if only because of their effect on the region's psychology about the future balance of power.

- China's ballistic missiles (including the carrier-killer DF-21 anti-ship ballistic missile), along with its less-heralded advanced cruise missiles, are ending the United States' previous advantage in precision strike systems.[17] As a result, U.S. ability and perceived willingness to project power forward in defense of allies and partners is likely to be increasingly called into question unless the United States finds effective responses. Attempts to identify "third offset strategies" are one response to the PLA's modernization trends.[18]

- Various other PLA developments include the rapid upgrade of its conventional forces, especially naval and air forces; the rapid expansion of its coast guard and white-hulled law enforcement vessels; and the development of offensive cyber and outer space capabilities.

- An even lower cost means of sea denial and control that could play in the Spratly Islands centers on China's development of contact, magnetic, acoustic, water pressure, remote control, and rocket rising mines. These mines, Navarro writes, citing Andrew Erickson and others, can be carried on China's 30,000 or so fishing trawlers or 50,000 or so other fishing craft.[19]

---

15. Sharon Chen, "Filipinos on South China Sea Isle Are Witness to Chinese Island Activities, Feel Threatened by Increasing Aggression," Bloomberg, July 13, 2015, http://www.japantimes.co.jp/news/2015/07/13/asia-pacific/filipinos-on-south-china-sea-isle-are-witness-to-chinese-island-activities-feel-threatened-by-increasing-aggression/?utm_source=rss&utm_medium=rss&utm_campaign=filipinos-on-south-china-sea-isle-are-witness-to-chinese-island-activities-feel-threatened-by-increasing-aggression.

16. Navarro, *Crouching Tiger*; also see Bernard D. Cole, *Asian Maritime Strategies: Navigating Troubled Waters* (Annapolis, MD: Naval Institute Press, 2013), 96–99.

17. Dennis M. Gormley, Andrew S. Erickson, and Jingdong Yuan, *A Low-Visibility Force Multiplier: Assessing China's Cruise Missile Ambitions* (Washington, DC: National Defense University Press, 2014), http://ndupress.ndu.edu/Portals/68/Documents/Books/force-multiplier.pdf.

18. For instance, see Deputy Secretary of Defense Robert Work, Speech to the Army War College Strategy Conference, April 8, 2015, http://www.defense.gov/utility/printitem.aspx?print=http://www.defense.gov/speeches/speech.aspx?speechid=1930.

19. Navarro, *Crouching Tiger*.

- China also appears to be bolstering its nuclear forces. Nuclear development is particularly opaque and there is a great debate over the size of China's nuclear arsenal. China is developing and deploying road-mobile intercontinental ballistic missiles (DF-31B) and a nuclear-powered strategic ballistic missile submarine (SSBN) fleet (with its *Jin*-class submarines, each with 16 missiles with up to four warheads each, able to reach some 7,500 miles). China is not only building newer, quieter, and more capable SSBNs (*Tang*-class Type 096 that may be able to reach the west coast of the United States from parts of the South China Sea) but also placing multiple reentry vehicles on warheads to achieve a second-strike capability. This becomes important even in peacetime because it could affect calculations of allies about the reliability of the U.S. deterrent and the fear of regional escalation.

Reflecting on the Military Balance in the South China Sea and U.S. and Regional Responses

Smaller states in the region have cause to be vigilant, if not anxious, about these trends. Diverse ASEAN members not surprisingly are showing various levels of anxiety in response to China's more assertive actions, including its island building and base building projects in the South China Sea. Surely, most governments in Southeast Asia are concerned when Chinese officials claim that their assertive actions are necessary to achieve a "China dream" and to protect their ancestors.[20] The United States' comprehensive rebalance to the Indo-Pacific region will and should focus on economic and political dimensions as much as military dimensions of power. It will also include an increasing focus on Southeast Asia within this vast region. Military presence and access, exercising and training, and capacity building for better situational awareness and assured access will all be part of the U.S. military posture aimed at preserving stability and underwriting core principles such as the rule of law and the peaceful resolution of disputes.

While this is a regional contest over rules and behavior, there are undeniably important questions about military and power balances. For instance, what about the shifting strategic military and power balance between China and the United States? Is China destined to become so powerful and the United States so weak that China's rise and China's revanchist behavior must be accommodated (on the argument, presumably, that accommodating provocative behavior will ensure that China behaves better in the future)?

The good news is that no major country seeks conflict or is spoiling for a fight. The bad news, however, is that the United States tends to invest in certain instruments of power with a narrow focus on winning decisive battles at the expense of thinking about less kinetic competitions. Sometimes this is expressed as the Chinese playing *weiqi* (*Go*, an

20. See Ben Blanchard, "China Says Changing Position on Sea Dispute Would Shame Ancestors," Reuters, June 27, 2015, http://www.reuters.com/article/2015/06/27/us-southchinasea-china-idUSKBN0P708U20150627; "China Headlines: How is the Chinese Dream Changing the World?," Xinhua, June 9, 2015, http://news.xinhuanet.com/english/china/2015-06/09/c_134311698.htm.

ancient Chinese strategy board game), while we play chess. If we overlook China's long-term strategy to strengthen its position and thereby maneuver the United States into losing options, we will have focused too much on military technology to the exclusion of political, economic, human, and psychological competition. Put differently, exquisite strategies can defeat exquisite military platforms.

This is why the United States must hew to a balanced approach of engaging, binding, and hedging. This approach must be comprehensive, beginning with strong economic foundations and active diplomatic and political engagement. A strong national military capability, and ever-stronger security cooperation with allies and new partners, will remain necessary to undergird this larger economic and political vision for a stable, prosperous, inclusive, rules-based region. We must keep our eye on this larger balance of power.

3 China's Island Building in the Spratly Islands

For What Purpose?

Bonnie S. Glaser[1]

The most prominent and problematic development in the South China Sea in the past two years is China's transformation of submerged or semisubmerged rocks and reefs into artificial islands. Since January 2014 Chinese vessels have dredged white sand and pumped it onto coral at seven features under its control in the disputed Spratly Islands: Fiery Cross Reef, Mischief Reef, Subi Reef, South Johnson Reef, Gaven Reef, Cuarteron Reef, and Hughes Reef. As islands are completed, China is erecting buildings, deploying troops, building harbors and airstrips, and installing radar and surveillance systems.

This frenetic building spree has aroused anxiety throughout the Asia-Pacific region. Much of the concern is due to fear about the purposes for which China will use the new islands and infrastructure, which are not completely clear. This is exacerbated by the fact that Beijing has yet to clarify the nature of its territorial and jurisdictional claims within its nine-dash line that covers more than 60 percent of the waters in the South China Sea.[2]

This paper begins by summarizing China's statements about its intentions regarding the artificial islands it is creating. It then examines the potential uses of these islands and discusses the threats that might be posed to regional stability. Finally, the paper makes recommendations about what steps might be taken to prevent or mitigate those threats.

---

1. The author is grateful to CSIS intern Emily Walz for research assistance in preparing this paper.

2. According to the U.S. Department of State, the exact percentage depends upon the assumed geographic extent of the South China Sea. The dashed line encompasses 62 percent of the waters in the South China Sea when using the limits that are described in the International Hydrographic Organization's (IHO) *S-23 Limits of the Oceans and Seas* (1953), which include the Taiwan Strait, the Gulf of Tonkin, and what is sometimes referred to as the Natuna Sea. U.S. Department of State, "China: Maritime Claims in the South China Sea," *Limits in the Seas* 143 (December 5, 2014), http://www.state.gov/documents/organization/234936.pdf.

China's Explanations Regarding the Purposes of Its Island Building

In mid-April 2015, China's Foreign Ministry for the first time provided an explanation for its large-scale island building in the South China Sea. Spokesperson Hua Chunying maintained that China's "maintenance and construction work" on its outposts in the Spratlys was aimed primarily at

> optimizing their functions, improving the living and working conditions of personnel stationed there, better safeguarding territorial sovereignty and maritime rights and interests, as well as better performing China's international responsibility and obligation in maritime search and rescue, disaster prevention and mitigation, marine science and research, meteorological observation, environmental protection, navigation safety, fishery production service and other areas.[3]

Upon completion of the construction, Hua maintained, the islands and reefs "would be able to provide all-round and comprehensive services to meet various civilian demands."[4] At the same time, however, she acknowledged that the islands would also "satisfy the need of necessary military defense."[5]

At the Shangri-La Dialogue in Singapore at the end of May, Admiral Sun Jianguo, China's representative, repeated the Foreign Ministry spokesperson's statement about the functions of the islands and reefs in the South China Sea. He added that an oceanic survey station for the United Nations has been built on Yongshu Jiao (Fiery Cross Reef), and that two multifunctional lighthouses are being constructed on Huayang Jiao (Cuarteron Reef) and Chigua Jiao (South Johnston Reef), for the "purpose of providing international public goods."[6]

Admiral Sun also noted that China intends to use the newly created islands to meet "necessary defense needs," but he did not articulate what those needs would be. China has evidently opted to say little about the defense purposes for which it plans to use the islands in the Spratlys. Possible reasons include:

- That the Chinese prefer to withhold this information for the time being;
- That final decisions have not yet been made; or
- Both of the above.

---

3. Foreign Ministry spokesperson Hua Chunying's regular press conference, April 9, 2015, http://www.fmprc.gov.cn/mfa_eng/xwfw_665399/s2510_665401/t1253488.shtml.
4. Ibid.
5. Ibid.
6. Admiral Sun Jianguo, Fourth Plenary Sessions, IISS Shangri-La Dialogue, May 31, 2015, https://www.iiss.org/en/events/shangri%20la%20dialogue/archive/shangri-la-dialogue-2015-862b/plenary4-b8e3/sun-0dfc.

China's ongoing construction on the artificial islands, its prior actions in the South China Sea, and comments by Chinese military experts provide some insights into the potential non-military purposes for which the new outposts might be used.

Sovereignty Assertion

FISHING IN DISPUTED WATERS

For China, economic and geopolitical strategies are entwined, as the defense of Chinese fishing fleets roaming further afield become a proxy for sovereignty claims, and a way to assert effective control over areas by denying access to other nations' civilians.[7] Chinese fishing fleets, part of the largest commercial fishing industry in the region, have moved away from China's overfished and polluted coasts, sailing in waters previously fished by other nations' fleets, which are now frequently barred from entry by Chinese law enforcement and military ships.

The creation of artificial islands in the Spratlys' fish-rich waters, which are several days' sail from mainland harbors, will allow Chinese fishing fleets to rest and refuel, further consolidating China's economic dominance, and by extension its de facto right to the area's resources. If foreign fishing fleets avail themselves of facilities on the newly created islands, this will further strengthen China's sovereignty claim.

For claimant nations, foreigners fishing in their territorial waters pose a challenge to sovereignty, and popular nationalist fervor pushes for harsher punishments for foreigners caught fishing "illegally," as well as pressure on states to protect their own fishers. Stepped-up maritime patrols from these newly built-up bases far from China's shores—particularly People's Liberation Army Navy (PLAN) frigates from the "forward naval station" at Mischief Reef, also a base for the People's Republic of China Fisheries Administration[8]—mean more government ships are on hand both to intimidate other nations' fishing fleets and to intervene when other nations' government vessels attempt to arrest Chinese fishers.[9]

An example of such Chinese intervention was seen in the Scarborough Shoal incident of 2012, where China's Fisheries Law Enforcement Command (FLEC) prevented the arrest of Chinese fishers, spotted by a Philippine maritime surveillance plane and found by a Philippine coast guard cutter to be holding marine harvests the Philippines declared illegal. The

7. Stephanie Kleine-Ahlbrandt, "Fish Story," *Foreign Policy*, June 25, 2012, http://foreignpolicy.com/2012/06/25/fish-story/; International Crisis Group, "Stirring up the South China Sea (II): Regional Responses," July 24, 2012, 13, http://www.crisisgroup.org/~/media/Files/asia/north-east-asia/229-stirring-up-the-south-china-sea-ii-regional-responses.pdf; and Beina Xu, "South China Sea Tensions," Council on Foreign Relations, May 14, 2014, http://www.cfr.org/china/south-china-sea-tensions/p29790.

8. Asia Maritime Transparency Initiative, "Island Tracker," CSIS, accessed August 27, 2015, http://amti.csis.org/mischief-reef/; Jaime Laude, "China Transforms Reef into Naval Station," *Philippine Star*, July 27, 2013, http://www.philstar.com/headlines/2013/07/27/1018091/china-transforms-reef-naval-station; and Andrew Chubb, "What's Not in the Latest Photos of China's Spratly Island Construction?," *South Sea Conversations*, February 25, 2015, https://southseaconversations.wordpress.com/2015/02/25/whats-not-in-the-latest-photos-of-chinas-spratly-island-construction/.

9. Xu, "South China Sea Tensions."

FLEC ships moved between the Philippine cutter and the fishing ships, beginning a standoff that ended when Manila withdrew its cutter and other vessels, and China occupied Scarborough Shoal.[10]

In addition to China's clashes with the Philippines, a similar scenario played out involving Chinese fishing vessels in waters claimed by Indonesia, which is not a formal claimant state to the disputed features in the South China Sea. Indonesia has on several occasions detained Chinese fishing boats caught in the waters off the Natuna Island group located within Indonesia's exclusive economic zone (EEZ), more than a thousand miles from the Chinese mainland. Chinese fishing boats under the protection of FLEC ships have entered into Natuna waters on multiple occasions, and have been detained by Indonesian vessels for illegal fishing.

In 2010 an Indonesian naval vessel detained 10 Chinese fishing boats, calling their entry into Indonesian waters "deliberate and coordinated." Armed FLEC ships were able to come to the fishing boats' aid within hours, prompting a standoff and the release of the vessels.[11] The ability of Chinese government ships to come quickly to the aid of fishing boats in far-flung portions of the South China Sea is another advantage of remote island outposts capable of hosting and refueling government fleets.

Chinese fishers enjoy not only tacit government approval to move into these faraway waters but outright encouragement and fuel subsidies reported at several thousand renminbi per day.[12] Reports allege that the government has also provided satellite radios using China's Beidou system to more than 50,000 fishing boats for Chinese citizens to call for help if they run into other nations' law enforcement.[13]

A more subtle provocation than military or government ships, fishing fleets enjoy the guise of non-military actors but nevertheless signal a national presence. Enjoying official backing and encouragement, Chinese fishing fleets have become a "maritime militia," or "surrogate navy," engaging with rival nations' fishing boats as part of a broader maritime offensive arsenal.[14] Major General Zhang Zhaozhong of the PLA popularized the "cabbage strategy"—surrounding a disputed area with a variety of vessels, from fishing boats to fishing administration ships to marine surveillance ships and navy warships, so that "the island is thus wrapped layer by layer like a cabbage."[15]

---

10. Alan Dupont, "Maritime Disputes in the South China Sea: ASEAN's Dilemma," in *Perspectives on the South China Sea: Diplomatic, Legal, and Security Dimensions of the Dispute*, ed. Murray Hiebert, Phuong Nguyen, and Gregory B. Poling (Washington, DC: CSIS, September 2014), 47, http://csis.org/files/publication/140930_Hiebert_PerspectivesSouthChinaSea_Web.pdf.

11. Ibid., 50.

12. John Ruwitch, "Satellites and Seafood: China Keeps Fishing Fleet Connected in Disputed Waters," Reuters, July 28, 2014, http://www.reuters.com/article/2014/07/28/us-southchinasea-china-fishing-insight-idUSKBN0FW0QP20140728.

13. Ibid.

14. Adam Pasick, "China Is Using Its Immense Commercial Fishing Fleet as a Surrogate Navy," *Quartz*, July 28, 2014, http://qz.com/241201/china-is-using-its-immense-commercial-fishing-fleet-as-a-surrogate-navy/.

15. Jeff Himmelman, "A Game of Shark and Minnow," *New York Times*, October 27, 2013, http://www.nytimes.com/newsgraphics/2013/10/27/south-china-sea/.

ENERGY ACTIVITY

An enhanced Chinese presence at the eastern and southern edges of the South China Sea would allow for more frequent and larger-scale disruption to energy exploration and drilling operations conducted by claimants in what China views as disputed waters. With shorter supply lines and more law enforcement vessels on station in the Spratlys, China will have more capability to interfere with such operations. In addition, it will have greater capability to defend its own oil rigs, which are increasingly being used to assert Chinese sovereignty in the waters of the South China Sea.

In recent years China has actively interfered with other nations' energy exploration in disputed waters. In 2011 China Marine Surveillance ships severed the cable towing sensors of a survey ship contracted by PetroVietnam.[16] China has also harassed ships in Reed Bank off the Philippines, nearly ramming a survey ship in 2011. In March 2015 the Philippine Department of Energy ordered energy companies to suspend work on current contracts pending resolution of the territorial dispute with China.[17] Also, in 2011 Beijing organized a flotilla of fishing vessels to block and ensnare a seismic survey vessel working for Talisman of Canada, which was awarded an exploration block by Hanoi near Vanguard Bank, approximately 650 nautical miles from the Chinese coast and 200 nautical miles from Vietnam.[18]

In May 2014 the state-owned China National Offshore Oil Corporation (CNOOC) moved the Haiyang Shiyou 981 drilling platform into disputed waters near the Paracel Islands, prompting rising tensions with Vietnam and anti-China riots in Vietnamese cities. In late June 2015 the rig was again positioned in waters where Chinese- and Vietnamese-claimed EEZs overlap, slightly further out from Vietnam's shores than the year prior.[19] In another incident that received little media attention, China dispatched another rig, the Haiyang 4, guarded by four escort vessels, to the area around Vanguard Bank, where it spent two weeks conducting seismic surveys.[20]

Potential Military Uses of China's Artificial Islands

ENHANCE MARITIME DOMAIN AWARENESS AND ISR

China's outposts in the Spratlys will undoubtedly be equipped with radar and electronic listening equipment that will enhance China's intelligence, surveillance, and

16. Carlyle A. Thayer, "Navigating the Currents of Legal Regimes and Realpolitik in East Asia's Maritime Domain," in *Securing the Safety of Navigation in East Asia: Legal and Political Dimension*, ed. Shicun Wu and Keyuan Zou (Cambridge, UK: Chandos, 2013), 32.

17. "Philippines Suspends Reed Bank Drilling in S. China Sea," Reuters, March 2, 2015, http://www.reuters.com/article/2015/03/03/philippines-southchinasea-philex-petrole-idUSL4N0W520F20150303.

18. "The South China Sea: Oil on Troubled Waters," *Economist*, January 25, 2015, http://www.businessinsider.com/the-south-china-sea-oil-on-troubled-waters-2015-1.

19. "China Moves Controversial Oil Rig Back towards Vietnam Coast," Reuters, June 26, 2015, http://www.reuters.com/article/2015/06/26/us-southchinasea-china-vietnam-idUSKBN0P60X320150626.

20. "The South China Sea: Oil on Troubled Waters."

reconnaissance (ISR) and maritime domain awareness capabilities in the South China Sea. The newly built runway on Fiery Cross Reef will enable China to operate maritime patrol as well as airborne warning and control system (AWACS) aircraft, if it chooses to do so. Depending on what platforms and systems are deployed on these outposts, China could have the ability to monitor most, if not all, of the South China Sea on a 24/7 basis. These enhanced capabilities will provide China with advantages over its weaker neighbors and pose challenges to U.S. military activities in the region.

INCREASE ANTI-ACCESS/AREA DENIAL AND POWER PROJECTION CAPABILITIES

China could deploy a wide variety of equipment, weapons, and platforms on its artificial islands, including radar, electronic listening equipment, surface-to-air missiles (SAMs), anti-ship cruise missiles (ASCMs), and manned and unmanned aircraft. In addition, the PLAN could station a small number of navy ships, possibly on a rotational basis. One or more runways in the Spratlys will support refueling operations for aircraft based on the mainland and Hainan Island, extending their operational ranges to encompass the entire South China Sea and beyond. One result will be an increased Chinese capability to observe and respond to U.S. military operations in the region. Essentially, China will be able to extend its anti-access/area denial (A2/AD) envelope farther southward and eastward, into the Philippines Sea and the Sulu Sea.

If a military conflict were to break out, the land features as well as the ships and aircraft operating from them would be vulnerable to attack, but in peacetime and a crisis, they will provide China with the capability to hold U.S. forces at risk at a farther distance than it can at present. This could have implications for a U.S. effort to come to Taiwan's defense. A U.S. carrier battle group sailing from the Arabian Gulf or Indian Ocean to come Taiwan's aid would have to pass through the South China Sea. In addition, in wartime, the need to attack these sites and the aircraft and ships deploying from them would divert U.S. assets from performing other missions.[21]

In the event that China decides to dislodge other claimants from their outposts, the PLA will have greater capability to do so. Helicopters, amphibious landing craft, and mobile artillery batteries could be used to conduct assaults on nearby land features. Alternatively, China could opt to put pressure on rival claimants to abandon some of their outposts. For example, it could attempt to disrupt resupply operations to isolated features that lack self-defense capability, such as Second Thomas Shoal, where a contingent of Philippine marines are stationed on a decaying World War II military ship. In early 2014 Chinese coast guard ships twice tried to block civilian Philippine vessels from resupplying the marines deployed on the shoal.[22]

---

21. Ben Dolven, Jennifer K. Elsea, Susan V. Lawrence, Ronald O'Rourke, and Ian E. Reinhart, "Chinese Land Reclamation in the South China Sea: Implications and Policy Options," Congressional Research Service, June 18, 2015, http://www.fas.org/sgp/crs/row/R44072.pdf.

22. Erik de Castro and Roli Ng, "Philippine Ship Dodges China Blockade to Reach South China Sea Outpost," Reuters, March 31, 2014, http://www.reuters.com/article/2014/03/31/us-philippines-china-reef-idUSBREA2U02720140331.

At least some Chinese military researchers have considered interfering with foreign resupply operations to force other claimants to abandon their outposts. Major General Zhang Zhaozhong warned, for example, "If we carry out the cabbage strategy, you will not be able to send food and drinking water onto the islands. Without the supply for one or two weeks, the troopers stationed there will leave the islands on their own. Once they have left, they will never be able to come back."[23]

With the ability to station greater numbers of large white-hulled vessels in the Spratlys, in some cases China might be able to successfully obstruct foreign resupply operations without using military ships. According to the U.S. Office of Naval Intelligence, "China prefers using its Coast Guard as the primary enforcer of its maritime claims. This approach limits the potential for confrontational incidents to escalate since most Chinese coast guard ships are unarmed, and those that are have relatively light weapons. This approach also helps Beijing manage the public optic of any enforcement actions."[24]

The new generation of coast guard cutters will reportedly be armed with 76-mm naval cannons, secondary gun turrets, anti-aircraft mounts, and be able to carry at least two multirole helicopters.[25] Such robustly armed cutters would allow the nominally non-military branch to more effectively intimidate other nations' military resupply runs. The Chinese coast guard 2901 is the first of a fleet of large 10,000-plus metric ton ships that are the world's largest cutters, featuring armed decks.[26] In confrontations where might makes right, these ships will give China an advantage, as the largest ships in any given confrontation are most likely to win games of brinkmanship.

ESTABLISH AN ADIZ

There has been much speculation that China intends to declare an air defense identification zone (ADIZ) in part or all of the area within its nine-dash line claim. An airstrip more than 10,000 feet long has been built on Fiery Cross Reef, which is big enough for virtually all China's aircraft, including fighter jets, transport planes, airborne early warning and control, and surveillance and tanker aircraft. According to one U.S. military commander, the runway and other military facilities on Fiery Cross could be operational as early as the end of 2015.[27]

This is China's second airstrip in the South China Sea, with the first located on Woody Island in the Paracels. In 2014 China began work on the Woody Island runway, expanding it from approximately 7,500 to 10,000 feet.

---

23. Himmelman, "A Game of Shark and Minnow."
24. U.S. Office of Naval Intelligence, "The PLA Navy," 2015, http://www.oni.navy.mil/Intelligence_Community/china_media/2015_PLA_NAVY_PUB_Print_Low_Res.pdf.
25. Tyler Rogoway, "Why China Is Building the World's Largest 'Coast Guard' Cutter," Foxtrot Alpha, January 6, 2015, http://foxtrotalpha.jalopnik.com/why-china-is-building-the-worlds-largest-coast-guard-1677699141.
26. Ryan D. Martinson, "East Asian Security in the Age of the Chinese Mega-Cutter," CIMSEC, July 3, 2015, http://cimsec.org/east-asian-security-age-chinese-mega-cutter/16974.
27. David Brunnstrom, "U.S. Vows to Continue Patrols after China Warns Spy Plane," Reuters, May 21, 2015, http://www.reuters.com/article/2015/05/21/us-southchinasea-usa-china-idUSKBN0O60AY20150521.

Satellite imagery from March 2015 indicates that China might be preparing to build yet another airstrip on Subi Reef, which would significantly increase its ability to monitor the large amount of airspace in the South China Sea. *IHS Jane's Defence Weekly* reported the existence of three landmasses created by dredgers that, if joined together, could create enough land for another 10,000-foot-long airstrip.[28] These runways, along with radar and refueling facilities to support operations by intercept aircraft, could increase China's capability to monitor and patrol an ADIZ. However, even with three airstrips and the help from radar, it would still be challenging for China to enforce an ADIZ that covers the entire airspace within its nine-dash line, especially the southernmost part of its claim.

In November 2013 China unilaterally set up an ADIZ in disputed waters in the East China Sea. At the time, a PLA major general confided that the Chinese military has long had plans to establish an ADIZ in China's near seas, including the East China Sea, Yellow Sea, and South China Sea.[29] Admiral Samuel Locklear, head of the U.S. Pacific Command, testified in April 2015 before Congress that the recent land reclamation in the Spratlys allows China "to exert basically greater influence over what's now a contested area. And it may be a platform if they ever wanted to establish an air defense identification zone."[30]

An ADIZ would require aircraft flying the zone to abide by Chinese-imposed rules, including the identification of flight plans, the presence of any transponders, and two-way radio communication with Chinese authorities. When it announced the East China Sea ADIZ, China's Ministry of National Defense (MND) also declared that it would adopt "emergency defensive measures" in response to aircraft that refuse to follow its rules.[31] Asked whether China planned to set up more air defense identification zones, for example, in the South China Sea, the MND spokesman replied, "After relevant preparation, China will set up other air defense identification zones at an appropriate time."[32]

In response to allegations that China has plans to establish an ADIZ in the South China Sea, China's Foreign Ministry spokesman said in February 2014 that "the Chinese side has yet to feel any air security threat from the ASEAN [Association of Southeast Asian Nations] countries and is optimistic about its relations with the neighboring countries and the general situation in the South China Sea region."[33] At the Shangri-La Dialogue, Admiral Sun Jianguo elaborated on this position, saying that "whether there is a plan to set up an

---

28. James Hardy and Sean O'Connor, "China's First Runway in Spratlys under Construction," *IHS Jane's Defence Weekly*, April 16, 2015, http://www.janes.com/article/50714/china-s-first-runway-in-spratlys-under-construction.

29. Private conversation, Washington, DC, December 2013.

30. J. Berkshire Miller, "China takes steps to control South China Sea," Al Jazeera, April 23, 2015, http://america.aljazeera.com/opinions/2015/4/china-takes-steps-to-control-south-china-sea.html.

31. Ministry of National Defense of the People's Republic of China, "Announcement of the Aircraft Identification Rules for the East China Sea Air Defense Identification Zone of the PRC," Xinhua, November 23, 2013, http://news.xinhuanet.com/english/china/2013-11/23/c_132911634.htm.

32. Mission of the People's Republic of China to the European Union, "Defense Ministry Spokesman Yang Yujun's Response to Questions of ADIZ at Regular Press Conference," November 28, 2013, http://www.chinamission.be/eng/more/zbzc/t1109759.htm.

33. "China Dismisses ADIZ Reports, Optimistic about South China Sea Situation," Xinhua, February 2, 2014, http://news.xinhuanet.com/english/china/2014-02/02/c_126085456.htm.

Air Defense Identification Zone depends on risks to our air safety and the degree of threat, as well as taking into consideration all aspects." He added that "overall, the current situation in the South China Sea is stable."[34]

Some voices in China are publicly calling for an ADIZ to be established. Senior Colonel Li Jie, a researcher at the PLAN's Military Academy and frequent media commentator, has insisted that "the establishment of another ADIZ over the South China Sea is necessary for China's long-term national interest."[35]

ESTABLISH SUBMARINE BASTION

Similar to the former Soviet Union's strategy in the Sea of Okhotsk in the Cold War, the island buildup could be an attempt to establish a defensive perimeter protecting an underground base for nuclear missile submarines at Yulin on the southern coast of Hainan Island.[36] The South China Sea's deep sea floor with underwater canyons could also provide a sanctuary where Chinese submarines could avoid detection. However, unlike the Sea of Okhotsk, the South China Sea contains major international shipping lanes, and would therefore be more difficult for the PLA to close off. Moreover, the JL-2 sea-launched ballistic missiles (SLBMs) carried by China's Type 094 nuclear-powered strategic ballistic missile submarine (SSBN) have an estimated range of approximately 4,600 miles, which means they cannot reach the west coast of the United States from the South China Sea.

To get within striking range of the United States, China's SSBNs would have to leave the bastion to go further out into the Philippine Sea, which would put them at risk of detection by antisubmarine warfare (ASW) operations conducted by the U.S. Navy and Japan's Maritime Self-Defense Force (MSDF). If China develops SLBMs with a greater range in the future, it would not need to move its submarines out of the South China Sea to strike the United States, and could then use the waters as a bastion.

Policy Recommendations

Calls for China to halt its artificial island building in the Spratlys have not been heeded. Completing the island projects as quickly as possible is apparently a high priority for Beijing, given the frenetic pace of dredging in the past year and half. However, there is still a possibility to put a cap on militarization of the islands by China and the other claimants. The deployment of offensive, power projection capabilities by any claimant would be dangerous and destabilizing. The United States should help to facilitate an agreement that

34. Sun Jianguo, IISS 14th Asia Security Summit/Shangri-La Dialogue Fourth Plenary Session Question & Answer, Singapore, May 31, 2015, https://www.iiss.org/en/events/shangri%20la%20dialogue/archive/shangri-la-dialogue-2015-862b/plenary4-b8e3/copy-of-qa-37d7.

35. Minnie Chan, "Southern Air Defense Zone 'Crucial for China in Long Term,' PLA Expert Says," *South China Morning Post*, February 22, 2014, http://www.scmp.com/news/china/article/1432938/southern-air-defence-zone-crucial-china-long-term-pla-expert-says.

36. Tetsuo Kotani, "Why China Wants South China Sea," *Diplomat*, July 18, 2011, http://thediplomat.com/2011/07/why-china-wants-the-south-china-sea/.

restricts deployments by all claimants to strictly defensive capabilities on all outposts in the South China Sea.

The growing uncertainty created by China's artificial island building and the purposes for which the new features will be used should motivate ASEAN members, or at least a subgroup of ASEAN members with deep interests in maritime security, to draw up a draft of a code of conduct that contains risk reduction measures and a dispute resolution mechanism. China is evidently unwilling to make progress with ASEAN on a code of conduct in a reasonable time frame and it is time for others to push this forward. If China and ASEAN are unprepared to finalize and sign a code of conduct then a coalition of the willing should proceed on its own and try to bring the others along later.

The United States should conduct freedom of navigation (FON) patrols around China's artificial islands that were originally submerged reefs. The United Nations Convention on the Law of the Sea (UNCLOS) provides that artificial islands do not qualify as "islands" under the convention because they are not naturally formed areas of land surrounded by and above water at high tide. Therefore, artificial islands are not entitled to any maritime zones. Since 1979 the United States has carried out the FON program to protect maritime rights through the world. Conducting such patrols in the Spratlys would signal China and the region of U.S. determination to ensure that disputes in the region are managed peacefully and in accordance with international law.

The United States should not exclude using its naval forces to deter China's continuing use of white-hulled paramilitary vessels to bully its smaller neighbors. By relying on paramilitary ships, China appears to believe that it can conduct coercive actions without incurring significant risk. This has caused anxiety throughout the region and provided China with an opportunity to change the status quo in its favor. A successful countercoercion strategy should entail consideration of greater acceptance of risk by demonstrating the United States' willingness to employ U.S. Navy ships in response to major Chinese provocations.

The United States and other nations should encourage Taiwan to clarify the meaning of its original 1947 map containing an 11-dash line and its territorial claim in the South China Sea. Because China's nine-dash line claim is based on Taiwan's original claim, a decision by Taiwan to clarify its claim would put pressure on Beijing to do the same. UNCLOS requires that maritime claims be derived from land features. It does not recognize "historical rights" as a basis for claiming EEZs or extended continental shelves.

The United States, Japan, Australia, and other willing nations should continue to assist the Philippines and Vietnam to enhance their maritime policing and defense capabilities so they can deter and respond to China entering the water and airspace in their EEZs with impunity. Similar help should be extended to Malaysia and Indonesia if requested.[37]

37. Some of these recommendations were previously put forward by the author in her testimony before the U.S.-China Economic and Security Review Commission Hearing on China's Relations with Southeast Asia, May 15, 2015, http://www.uscc.gov/sites/default/files/Glaser_Written%20Testimony_5.13.2015%20Hearing.pdf.

Increased maritime domain awareness by all nations in the region can help to deter others from taking provocative and destabilizing actions.

Finally, the sovereignty dispute over land features in the South China Sea should ideally be brought to the International Court of Justice, but this is unlikely to happen. Therefore, a reasonable approach would be for all the claimants to accept the doctrine of international law known as Uti Possidetis Juris, which means "as you possess under law."[38] In other words, the status quo should be accepted by all. Then an agreement should be reached on the maritime zones to which the various land features are entitled based on UNCLOS. This would lay the groundwork for agreement on cooperative projects in the high seas—waters that are not part of the territorial seas—involving energy, counterpiracy, scientific and meteorological investigation, and other areas.

38. Charles W. Freeman Jr., "Diplomacy on the Rocks: China and Other Claimants in the South China Sea," Remarks at a seminar of the Watson Institute for International Studies, Brown University, Providence, RI, April 10, 2015, http://chasfreeman.net/diplomacy-on-the-rocks-china-and-other-claimants-in-the-south-china-sea/.

4 Developments in the South China Sea

Perspectives on the Philippines, Malaysia, and Beyond

Bill Hayton

It is best to begin with what this paper does not focus on: namely the discussions on an Association of Southeast Asian Nations (ASEAN)–China regional code of conduct in the South China Sea. These talks have been going on, in different guises, since 1995, after China occupied Mischief Reef. So far ASEAN and China have agreed on a Declaration on the Conduct of Parties in the South China Sea (DOC) in 2002, the creation of an ASEAN-China Joint Working Group on the Implementation of the DOC in 2004,[1] and most recently, Guidelines for the Implementation of the DOC in July 2011.

Yet in spite of 20 years of talks, the two sides have not been able to find agreement on concrete measures to control activities in the South China Sea. In short, China is not going to agree to anything that limits its freedom of action and there is no point in ASEAN agreeing to anything that does not limit China's freedom of action. So there are three possible outcomes to the ongoing talks: they collapse, they result in another pointless piece of paper, or they go on forever—providing much needed state subsidies to the luxury hotels of Southeast Asia. The best that can be said for the process is, to paraphrase Winston Churchill, "Jaw-jaw is better than war-war."

Neither does this paper explore China's Twenty-First Century Maritime Silk Road Initiative in depth. So far, for Southeast Asia at least, that seems to be another example of jaw-jaw. It has been nearly two years since President Xi Jinping announced the initiative and the only things seen so far are yet more subsidies for luxury hotels: a few conferences and banquets but not a single yuan invested anywhere outside China. The only concrete initiative to have emerged under its rubric is the signing of letters of intent between Malaysia's formerly corruption-riddled Port Klang Authority and five Chinese ports. While there is no doubt that most ASEAN states have desperate need of infrastructure investment, it is not yet clear that the Maritime Silk Road will deliver it.

1. Carlyle Thayer, "China-ASEAN and the South China Sea: Chinese Assertiveness and Southeast Asian Responses," in *Major Law and Policy Issues in the South China Sea: European and American Perspectives*, ed. Yann-huei Song and Keyuan Zou (Burlington, VT: Ashgate, 2014), 44.

So long as ASEAN perceives China's activities in the South China Sea as threatening, its member states are likely to treat such initiatives with caution. In 2014 China proposed making 2015 the Year of China-ASEAN Maritime Cooperation, and in March the year was formally launched on the sidelines of the Boao Forum.[2] Since then the silence has been deafening. The China-ASEAN Maritime Cooperation Fund was announced with much fanfare at the 14th China-ASEAN summit in November 2011 with a $500 million budget but does not appear to have disbursed any significant funds outside China. The China-ASEAN Maritime Partnership was proposed by Premier Wen Jiabao at the 15th China-ASEAN summit the following year.[3] Again, nothing has come of it. ASEAN has declined to participate; there is no cooperation.

Instead, this paper focuses on how the events of the past year—particularly the international reaction to China's construction of seven artificial islands and the start of legal proceedings at the Permanent Court of Arbitration—have created an opportunity for peace in the South China Sea. Yes, peace.

As is generally understood, there are two sets of disputes in the South China Sea. There are small arguments about which country first stuck its flag in which island or reef. And there are big arguments about whether countries should stick to the regime of international law that has, over the past 70 years, created the most peaceful and prosperous era in world history. Resolutions to both are within grasp, if the players choose to reach for them.

Before explaining how, it is worth noting that concern about the wider implications of the South China Sea situation for the current rules-based international order is spreading. Even the European Union—despite plenty of other problems on its plate at the moment—is raising its concerns. At the 2015 Shangri-La Dialogue, its high representative for foreign policy, Federica Mogherini, specifically referenced a maritime order based on international law, including the United Nations Convention on the Law of the Sea (UNCLOS):

> We need to maintain a maritime order based on international law, including the UN Convention on the Law of the Sea. We are not getting into the legitimacy of specific claims, but we are resolute as Europeans on HOW they should be resolved—that is, peacefully, without the use or threat of force.[4]

---

2. Prashanth Parameswaran, "China's Plan for ASEAN-China Maritime Cooperation," *Diplomat*, April 1, 2015, http://thediplomat.com/2015/04/chinas-plan-for-asean-china-maritime-cooperation/.

3. Bao Haibin, "China-ASEAN Maritime Cooperation Fund," PowerPoint presentation at the ASEAN Regional Forum Maritime Security Workshop on Preparedness and Response to Marine Pollution Incidents, Honolulu, HI, March 4–5, 2014, http://aseanregionalforum.asean.org/files/Archive/21st/ARF%20Maritime%20Security%20Workshop%20on%20Preparedness%20and%20Response%20to%20Marine%20Pollution%20Incidents,%20Honolulu,%204-5%20March%202014/Annex%209%20-%20China-ASEAN%20Maritime%20Cooperation%20Fund.pdf.

4. Federica Mogherini, Speech at the 14th IISS [International Institute for Strategic Studies] Asia Security Summit/Shangri-La Dialogue, Singapore, May 31, 2015, http://eeas.europa.eu/statements-eeas/2015/150531_02_en.htm.

With the European Union, the United States, and Japan all concerned about these issues, it is no surprise that the Group of Seven (G7), has also taken them up.[5] In April it published its first ever "Declaration on Maritime Security," which included specific mention of the East China Sea and South China Sea and a statement that the group is:

> concerned by any unilateral actions, such as large scale land reclamation, which change the status quo and increase tensions. We strongly oppose any attempt to assert territorial or maritime claims through the use of intimidation, coercion or force.[6]

The statement did not, however, mention any countries by name.

Australia's defense minister, Kevin Andrews, also used the Shangri-La Dialogue to make clear his government's "opposition to any coercive or unilateral actions to change the status quo in the South and East China Sea [including] any large scale land reclamation activity."[7] And Canberra demonstrated its unhappiness by inviting Japanese troops to the annual U.S.-Australian Talisman Sabre military exercise. In both 2014 and 2015 Australia also took part in the annual U.S.-Philippines Balikatan exercises. Australia is about to transfer two tank landing craft to the Philippines.

Completing the triangle, the Philippines and Japan held their first-ever joint naval exercises in the South China Sea in mid-May 2015, following an agreement between the two countries signed in January.[8] Japan is delivering 10 patrol ships to the Philippine coast guard and committed to upgrade Manila's surveillance and defense capacities. In June the two countries formalized their strategic partnership.[9]

India has grown more involved too. In September 2014 an India-U.S. joint statement specifically mentioned the South China Sea for the first time. President Barack Obama and Prime Minister Narendra Modi called for the resolution of the territorial and maritime disputes, "in accordance with universally recognized principles of international law, including UNCLOS."[10]

India has ignored Chinese objections and again invited Japan to take part in its annual Malabar naval exercises, with the United States, in October 2015. India, Japan, and the United States will also hold their trilateral dialogue at the ministerial level for the first

5. The G7 includes Canada, France, Germany, Italy, Japan, the United Kingdom, and the United States.

6. G7 Foreign Minister' Declaration on Maritime Security, Lübeck, Germany, April 15, 2015, http://www.auswaertiges-amt.de/EN/Infoservice/Presse/Meldungen/2015/150415_G7_Maritime_Security.html.

7. Kevin Andrews, Speech at the 14th IISS Asia Security Summit/Shangri-La Dialogue, Singapore, May 31, 2015, http://kevinandrews.com.au/latest-news/2015/05/31/114th-iiss-asia-security-summit-the-shangri-la-dialogue/.

8. Reuters, "Japan Steps Up Maritime Engagement with Philippines, Vietnam," InterAksyon, May 12, 2015, http://www.interaksyon.com/article/110424/japan-steps-up-maritime-engagement-with-philippines-vietnam.

9. Associated Press, "Philippines Wants Defense Pact for Japanese Troops," *New York Times*, June 5, 2015, http://www.nytimes.com/aponline/2015/06/05/world/asia/ap-as-japan-philippines-military.html.

10. White House, "U.S.-India Joint Statement," September 30, 2014, https://www.whitehouse.gov/the-press-office/2014/09/30/us-india-joint-statement.

time on the sidelines of the 2015 East Asia Summit. There are also separate India-Japan naval exercises.

All around the region, security arrangements that used to be characterized as hub and spoke—with the United States as the hub—are also becoming peer-to-peer networks. Australia, India, Japan, the Philippines, South Korea, Vietnam, and others are gradually building new, direct security and diplomatic relations with each other. There are some exceptions—only the "I" in BRICS has spoken, for example—but almost every other major country has, directly or indirectly, criticized China's island building and made specific calls for the principles of UNCLOS to be applied.[11]

This brings us to The Hague, Netherlands, and the Palace of Peace—the seat of the Permanent Court of Arbitration—where the first hearings in the Philippines' case against China were heard in early July 2015.[12] The tribunal first has to decide whether to hear the case, which is really a question of whether it thinks that the territorial disputes need to be resolved before it can make a ruling based on UNCLOS about what kind of maritime zones can be claimed from each feature. Assuming the tribunal decides to hear the case—and it would be surprising if it does not—then the Philippines can be expected to win on almost every count.

Of the seven Chinese-occupied features in the Spratlys, four contain rocks that remain above water at high tide and three would be submerged in their natural state. Neither they nor Scarborough Shoal can support human habitation. Therefore they generate a 12-nautical-mile territorial sea, at best, and absolutely no exclusive economic zone (EEZ) at all.

So it is highly likely that the effect of the Philippines' case will be for the tribunal to rule China's U-shaped, or nine-dash, line incompatible with international law. Many are already asking, "So what? China will just ignore the ruling." But think of this scenario.

The Philippines needs to exploit new reserves of natural gas to replace its Malampaya field off the coast of Palawan. Malampaya, which is operated by Shell in partnership with Chevron and the Philippine National Oil Co. (PNOC), currently provides about a third of the electricity used on the main island of Luzon including the capital, Manila. Coverage in the Philippine media suggests the field will run out by 2024.[13]

Seismic surveys suggest the answer lies under the Reed Bank, which lies within the nine-dash line. Surveys commissioned by Forum Energy projected gas reserves there of 8.8 trillion cubic feet—larger than Malampaya.[14] Given that it took six years to develop the

11. BRICS stands for "Brazil, Russia, India, China, and South Africa."
12. "See U in Court," *Economist*, July 16, 2015, http://www.economist.com/news/asia/21657807-tribunal-ponders-chinas-claims-see-u-court.
13. Alvin Elchico, "Natural Gas Supply at Malampaya to Last until 2024," ABS-CBN News, October 21, 2014, http://www.abs-cbnnews.com/business/10/21/14/natural-gas-supply-malampaya-last-until-2024.
14. Chris Larano, "Philex to Send Survey Ship to Disputed Reed Bank," *Wall Street Journal*, October 29, 2014, http://www.wsj.com/articles/philex-to-send-survey-ship-to-disputed-reed-bank-1414584594.

original Malampaya project (from the discovery of commercial-sized gas reserves in 1995 until the inauguration of the project in 2001), the need to begin drilling and pipeline construction is pressing if the Philippine capital is to avoid electricity shortages in less than a decade. However, in March, Forum Energy announced that the Philippine government had denied it permission to drill because of objections from China. Since then Forum Energy has been forced to delist its shares from the London Stock Exchange.[15]

However, if the Permanent Court of Arbitration were to rule that China has no legitimate EEZ claim on the resources of the Reed Bank, then the Philippines would be able to argue that any gas extraction activity by Forum Energy, or another company operating under a Philippine license, is entirely lawful. If China tried to obstruct such lawful activity then it would be easy for its critics to term its actions a violation of international law. This would be the perfect opportunity for the United States, if it so chose, to draw a line in the sea.

There would be issues to clarify regarding the geographic scope of the United States' commitment to protect the Philippines under the U.S.-Philippines Mutual Defense Treaty, but since Article V of the treaty includes reference to "armed forces, public vessels or aircraft in the Pacific," it should not be difficult for government lawyers to argue that it includes the South China Sea.[16] This could also be the occasion when other countries that have chosen to speak out in support of the existing maritime order come to the defense of UNCLOS and add their diplomatic and other support to the efforts of the United States and the Philippines. This would be a dangerous moment—China and the United States, and possibly other states, could go eyeball to eyeball around the Reed Bank. But at this point, China would probably have to blink. It is not likely to come out well from such a confrontation.

The question is whether China is willing to risk the consequences of that confrontation, which could be as little as two years away, or whether it can see the writing on the wall now and start to take steps to prevent it from happening. In essence the question is this: does the Chinese political leadership regard its interests in the South China Sea as so important that they are worth damaging its other international relationships? If the leadership does not, then can the central interest of the Chinese party-state as a whole outweigh those of the various state agencies—military, coastguard, oil companies, fishing lobbies, and coastal provinces—with their own bureaucratic agendas to advance?

The root cause of these agencies' actions in the South China Sea is the version of history that has become orthodoxy in Chinese primary schools and Communist Party academies, in which the sea has been under Chinese jurisdiction "since ancient times." I would argue that too many analyses of the disputes pay too little attention to the seriousness with which China regards its historical claim. I have argued elsewhere that this version of history is

---

15. "Forum Energy Discloses Plans to Delist Shares from UK Exchange," BusinessWorld, April 20, 2015, http://www.bworldonline.com/content.php?section=Corporate&title=forum-energy-discloses-plans-to-delist-shares-from-uk-exchange&id=106458.

16. "Mutual Defense Treaty between the United States and the Republic of the Philippines," August 30, 1951, Article V, http://avalon.law.yale.edu/20th_century/phil001.asp.

based upon misreadings of evidence, misinterpretations, and even mistranslations.[17] Nonetheless, it is a critical motivating factor behind Chinese actions in the sea. It deserves much more attention.

This warped version of history lies behind China's most recent attempt to expand its territorial control in the South China Sea: at the Luconia Shoals, about 65 nautical miles off the coast of Borneo. In early June 2015 Shahidan Kassim, the Malaysian minister with responsibility for his country's coast guard, posted on Facebook pictures from an inspection flight over the shoals and, in a news conference at Miri Airport in nearby Sarawak State, revealed that a Chinese coast guard vessel had been at anchor at Luconia Shoals since August 2013.

The origins of China's expedition to this reef are bizarre. China's original claim to the Spratlys and nearby reefs arose from meetings of a Republic of China government committee back in 1935. No Chinese official had ever visited the Spratlys at this point, so the Inspection Committee of Land and Water Maps simply took the existing British maps and translated or transliterated the names into Chinese. Luconia is not a Chinese name, it is an old term for Luzon.[18]

In 1935 the Inspection Committee simply transliterated the English name Luconia as Lo Kang Ni A Tan [南盧康尼亞灘]—where *tan* is the Chinese word for "sandbank." It was not until 1947 that Republic of China officials decided to give the features more "Chinese" names. They chose Bei-kang Ansha [北康暗沙] for the northern and Nan-kang Ansha [南康暗沙] for the southern parts of the shoals. *Kang* [康] literally means "health" but it is more likely that it was simply an abbreviation of the earlier transliteration. The word *an-sha* (literally "hidden sand") seems to have been borrowed from literature at around this time to provide a Chinese linguistic equivalent to the English word "shoal"—an obscure nautical term derived from an Old English word meaning "shallow."[19]

The oft-made assertion that China was the "first to name" the islands of the South China Sea simply is not supported by the evidence. However, China's sense of entitlement to the Spratly Islands, based on equally un-evidenced assertions, has become the greatest danger to peace in the South China Sea. The continuing miseducation about China's historical claims only generates a sense of grievance among the population that makes the disputes so much more difficult to resolve.

Andrew Chubb's blog, *South Sea Conversations*, provides some of the more recent background on China's attempts to occupy the Luconia Shoals.[20] It seems to have begun with a

---

17. See, for example, Bill Hayton, "Fact, Fiction and the South China Sea," *Asia Sentinel*, May 25, 2015, http://www.asiasentinel.com/politics/fact-fiction-south-china-sea/; Bill Hayton, "China's False Memory Syndrome," *Prospect Magazine*, July 10, 2014, http://www.prospectmagazine.co.uk/world/chinas-false-memory-syndrome.

18. Bill Hayton, *The South China Sea: The Struggle for Power in Asia* (New Haven, CT: Yale University Press, 2014).

19. Ibid.

20. Andrew Chubb, "Luconia Breakers: China's New 'Southernmost Territory' in the South China Sea?," *South Sea Conversations*, June 16, 2015, https://southseaconversations.wordpress.com/2015/06/16/luconia-breakers-chinas-new-southernmost-territory-in-the-south-china-sea/.

trip to the shoals by a trio from *Chinese National Geography* magazine aboard Malaysian boats in April/May 2009. The whole story can be read on Chubb's blog, but it does seem possible that the expedition put an idea in the heads of China's State Oceanic Administration—persuading them to try and claim the shoals as the country's new southernmost territory.

Chinese coast guard vessels appear to have been on almost permanent station at Luconia Shoals and the nearby James Shoal since 2013. This is in addition to less regular visits by passing Chinese naval flotillas. There have also been reports of Chinese vessels interfering with Malaysian oil surveys in the same area. Two took place in mid-August 2012[21] and others subsequently.

China's actions have caused Malaysia to adjust its previous attitude of "keep quiet and trust in the special relationship with Beijing." Prime Minister Najib Razak personally criticized China's island building in the run-up to the ASEAN summit in April 2015.[22] Despite early indications that Malaysia would try to steer ASEAN away from confrontation with China,[23] ASEAN was resolute under Malaysia's chairmanship in its opposition to China's recent actions. The summit conclusions were forthright, noting that China's island building had "eroded trust and confidence and may undermine peace, security and stability in the South China Sea."[24] Sources also suggest that Malaysian officials have been working more closely with their counterparts from Vietnam and the Philippines, both in developing common positions on the sea disputes within ASEAN and as a trio vis-à-vis China.

They may not say so publicly, but privately these countries have, in essence, reached a common position on the territorial disputes. They point to the language in the 2002 ASEAN-China DOC about not "resorting to the threat or use of force" to demonstrate that they have no plans to expel other Southeast Asian claimants from the features they occupy.[25] In other words, de facto, they respect the legitimacy of the existing island and reef occupations. They may not be prepared to give formal de jure recognition of those occupations, but it is clear that, within ASEAN at least, territorial disputes in the Spratlys are barely an issue.

Could the same de facto understanding be extended to China?

---

21. James Clad and Robert A. Manning, "China's Bad Diplomacy," *National Interest*, December 17, 2012, http://nationalinterest.org/commentary/chinas-bad-diplomacy-7855?page=show.

22. "Najib: Avoid Show of Force in Maritime Overlapping Claims," *Borneo Post*, April 24, 2015, http://www.theborneopost.com/2015/04/24/najib-avoid-show-of-force-in-maritime-overlapping-claims/.

23. Praveen Menon and Manuel Mogato, "Host Malaysia Avoids Chinese Ire over Disputed Sea at ASEAN Summit," Reuters, April 23, 2015, http://www.reuters.com/article/2015/04/23/us-asean-summit-philippines-idUSKBN0NE0TL20150423.

24. "South China Sea Island-Building 'May Undermine Peace'—ASEAN," BBC, April 28, 2015, http://www.bbc.com/news/world-asia-32476951.

25. Declaration on the Conduct of Parties in the South China Sea, Phnom Penh, November 4, 2002, http://www.asean.org/asean/external-relations/china/item/declaration-on-the-conduct-of-parties-in-the-south-china-sea.

All that is required for peace in the South China Sea is for all the claimants to recognize the occupations of the others and to declare unequivocally that they subscribe to the spirit and letter of UNCLOS. There will be losses of course, but also gains. Vietnam will lose the Paracel Islands but it will gain legitimacy in the Spratlys and, with the end of the nine-dash line, it will be able to exploit hydrocarbons and fish without confrontation. China will lose the nine-dash line but it will gain legitimacy in the Paracels, on the features that it occupies in the Spratlys, and, more importantly, drastically reduce the potential for confrontation with the United States. The Philippines will lose its claim to the parts of the Kalayaan Island group—the large area of the Spratlys it claims—that it does not occupy, but will gain the Reed Bank and an undisputed EEZ along its coastlines. All of the pieces are in place; it is really up to China now.

5 The International Community and the Strategic Balance in the South China Sea

Peter Jennings

The South China Sea faces increasingly sharp-edged strategic competition involving claimant states and major powers with interests in the region. There is an absence of an effective strategic balance in the region and of mechanisms to help create a balance. In this vacuum there is a jumble of competing interests among states that have different capacities and different levels of motivation to shape outcomes. The challenge for the international community is to decide how to try moderating Chinese behavior when Beijing is the most motivated actor and when other powers either lack the capacity or are reluctant to directly engage in the dispute. The South China Sea lacks options for a solution to strategic competition because of this asymmetry of motive and capability.

Competition in the South China Sea also plays out in a wider strategic context of the growth of Chinese influence and of relations between the major powers. If the broad sweep of relations between China and the United States is positive, that could result in Washington being reluctant to challenge Chinese behavior in the South China Sea. The same logic applies to the responses of other countries with interests in the region. Thus China pragmatically strengthens its position in the South China Sea by testing the limits of international tolerance for its island construction and other activities. So far the obvious conclusion seems to be that China is indeed able to make gains for little or no practical penalty.

This paper assesses the mix of motivations and capabilities that shape the behavior of countries with interests in the South China Sea. It asks what steps the international community could take to develop a more effective response to Chinese behavior aimed at keeping the region stable.

China

China's actions in the South China Sea show a significant intensification of effort in island building and in maintaining a substantial military and paramilitary patrolling presence at sea and in the air. Its efforts in the region reflect a broader set of strategic priorities: to strengthen maritime force projection capability; to raise the level of difficulty and cost to any opposing military force operating in the region; and to broaden options open to the People's Liberation Army (PLA) in any future contingency.

That said, there appears to be a strong element of opportunism in China's approach. While there is no denying the planning and logistic effort required to build some 2,000 acres of land in a remote and difficult operating area, it is more difficult to see the long-term military utility of such outposts. They would be very exposed in a heightened conflict, presenting serious sustainment and protection challenges, and able to provide only limited support to PLA operations.

Chinese claims that the construction is to support counterpiracy roles and to facilitate humanitarian assistance and disaster relief (HADR) lack credibility. To the extent that there is a piracy problem in the region it is hundreds of miles to the southwest, in the approaches to the Strait of Malacca. The reclaimed islands are themselves most likely to need HADR support because of their exposure to the frequent hurricanes in the region. The most obvious strategic utility of the island construction is simply to assert Chinese presence in peacetime. No country has the interest to physically remove the Chinese presence because to do so would be to dramatically escalate the dispute. Having created facts on the ground, the physical reality of Chinese presence is a far more effective demonstration of Chinese sovereignty than resorting to the spurious legal validity of the nine-dash line.

Beyond any strategic calculation of the value of the South China Sea, China's activities in the region also reflect political and emotional goals. The reclamation activity fits well with the more assertive national maritime approach articulated by President Xi Jinping and set out most recently in the May 2015 white paper, "China's Military Strategy": moving the PLA Navy (PLAN) from an "offshore water defense" role to one of "open seas protection."[1] This more assertive approach plays well to popular nationalist sentiment. China is island building because it can and because such an assertion of strength is welcomed by a people schooled in the history of China's weakness and mistreatment by international powers.

It is difficult to escape the conclusion that China's more assertive push in the South China Sea is motivated by a calculation that it can get away with it, both in terms of regional and great power reactions. The relatively low-key and brief global reaction against China's November 2013 declaration of an East China Sea air defense identification zone (ADIZ) may have encouraged Chinese planners to begin the intensified land reclamation effort in 2014. In terms of regional diplomacy, China has ignored criticism from the smaller claimant states, in part by openly dismissing their views: "small countries shouldn't make unreasonable demands" was the Chinese Ministry of Foreign Affairs' public comment in

1. State Council Information Office of the People's Republic of China, "China's Military Strategy," May 2015, http://news.usni.org/2015/05/26/document-chinas-military-strategy.

January 2015.[2] Private diplomacy has at times been contemptuous of Association of Southeast Asian Nations (ASEAN) countries.

U.S. public diplomacy in reaction to China's land reclamation has certainly expressed clear opposition to the activity. At the May 2015 Shangri-La Dialogue in Singapore, for example, U.S. secretary of defense Ashton Carter made a strong call for a halt to land reclamation and militarization of features on the part of all claimant states.[3] This had earlier been reinforced by the May 27, 2015, flight of a U.S. P-8 maritime surveillance aircraft over Fiery Cross Reef. Any international follow-up to assert air or maritime access in the South China Sea has been either very low key or nonexistent. China's ambiguous response to U.S. efforts was to say in June that it would soon "complete" its reclamation efforts but then continue to build facilities on the islands.[4] There was no clear indication of a lessening of Chinese activity and any that did occur may have been little more than a tactical delay in anticipation of President Xi Jinping's visit to the United States in September.

The Other Claimant States

Of the Southeast Asian countries, Brunei, Malaysia, the Philippines, and Vietnam maintain claims to different features of overlapping areas of the South China Sea. The Philippines and Vietnam have increasingly strained relations with China as a result of the latter's assertive actions at sea, and diplomatically due to competing claims. While the particularities of each country's claims and responses differ, Southeast Asian claimants share a sense of being affronted by China's, at times undisguised, dismissal of the concerns of smaller countries. The smaller claimant states lack significant military or paramilitary assets to respond to Chinese behavior. This lack of capacity underpins a region-wide turning to the United States.

The tendency of some claimant and non-claimant Southeast Asian states to want to get closer to the United States as a result of a more assertive Chinese approach might indicate that Beijing's policy is in fact counterproductive. Surely there is more value to Beijing in sustaining positive relations with ASEAN member states than in asserting absolute control over the rocks, islets, and concrete platforms of the South China Sea? In fact, it may be that Beijing calculates there is greater immediate value in controlling the rocks. ASEAN does not look as though it is developing a capacity for concerted response to Chinese action at any time soon. China has worked very hard to make sure that ASEAN member states

---

2. Ministry of Foreign Affairs of the People's Republic of China, "Foreign Ministry Spokesperson Hua Chunying's Regular Press Conference," January 22, 2015, http://www.fmprc.gov.cn/mfa_eng/xwfw_665399/s2510_665401/t1230645.shtml.

3. Ashton Carter, "The United States and Challenges of Asia-Pacific Security," Speech at the 14th IISS [International Institute for Strategic Studies] Asia Security Summit/Shangri-La Dialogue, Singapore, May 30, 2015, https://www.iiss.org/en/events/shangri%20la%20dialogue/archive/shangri-la-dialogue-2015-862b/plenary1-976e/carter-7fa0.

4. "China to 'Complete' South China Sea Land Reclamation," BBC News, June 16, 2015, http://www.bbc.com/news/world-asia-china-33144751.

struggle to hold and articulate a common position on the South China Sea. The territorial claims also have to be weighed against the totality of relations with China, which is among the largest trading partners of each Southeast Asian country. China has been prepared to use economic pressure against Asian countries in attempting to securing diplomatic leverage as well. In short, claimant states have solid reasons not to want to risk their broader China relationships even as their positions are being eroded by the growth of a stronger Chinese presence on the disputed features.

Even if Vietnam and the Philippines do develop closer defense relations with the United States, it is not obvious that these ties will translate into effective responses at sea to Chinese claims. For its part, Washington will not want to create an impression in Manila or Hanoi that closer military ties automatically draw the United States into more support for either party's claims. China's position does not win it friends in the region, but claimant states try not to completely alienate Beijing out of concern not to damage broader relations.

An exception to the generally cautious approach of the smaller claimants is the Philippines, which has pursued its high profile case at the Permanent Court of Arbitration at The Hague. The final legal outcome from this process is some time away. While the outcome will be significant in terms of international legal judgments, China's actions make it clear that it is not going to participate in the process or acknowledge its outcome, and will continue to take practical steps in the region to assert its control. In this sense the international legal position lags significantly behind the reality of actions on the ground and has therefore not provided a responsive means to manage or moderate the dispute.

Taiwan's position as a claimant state differs from that of the Southeast Asian claimants, in as much as Beijing regards the country as a province and therefore subsumes Taiwan's claims into its own. Taiwan has sought to make its own claims potentially more palatable to the international community by—somewhat bizarrely—offering a solar-powered five-bed hospital on Itu Aba (Taiping) Island for international humanitarian aid purposes.[5] Taiwan's position is low key and clearly of less immediate concern to other countries. The January 2016 presidential and legislative elections in Taiwan may produce a more sharply differentiated handling strategy on island claims, depending on the outcomes.

Non-Claimant States

As a non-claimant state, Singapore attempts to use its leverage within ASEAN to encourage a more concerted regional approach to dealing with China. It also works hard to sustain an international focus on the region. The annual Shangri-La Dialogue, for example, has become a key vehicle to bring senior defense officials to the region and encourage a dialogue on key strategic issues. In 2015 the South China Sea was the meeting's single biggest focus, displaying both the strengths and limitations to regional engagement.

5. Associated Press, "Taiwan Promotes its Island Claim in South China Sea," *New Zealand Herald*, July 18, 2015, http://www.nzherald.co.nz/world/news/article.cfm?c_id=2&objectid=11483259&ref=rss.

A clear strength of the Shangri-La Dialogue is that it forces the region to hold a public and senior level discussion about the South China Sea. It was not coincidental that Secretary Carter's speech calling for a halt to reclamation and demilitarization was preceded a few days before the dialogue by the P-8 aircraft flight. The dialogue also produced a series of statements by defense ministers, including from Australia, Germany, Japan, and Malaysia, all stressing the importance of unfettered air and sea transit rights through the region. A customarily nuanced keynote address from Lee Hsien Loong, the prime minister of Singapore, made clear the risks to regional stability if strategic competition is not moderated. The challenge, he said, is to "resist the temptation to be consumed by short-term issues, [and to] keep our focus on longer-term shared interests."[6]

Unfortunately the Shangri-La Dialogue also showed the current limits to the international community's response to the South China Sea. For a start, both the United States and Japan appeared to offer separate and uncoordinated plans for enhancing maritime security. In the case of the United States this was a $425 million Southeast Asia maritime security initiative to be run by the U.S. Department of Defense encouraging maritime capacity-building efforts.[7] The second proposal came from Gen Nakatani, the Japanese minister of defense, for what he called The Shangri-La Dialogue Initiative consisting of promoting maritime confidence-building measures for navies to prevent incidents at sea, shared maritime domain awareness, and more collaborative HADR responses.[8] Both initiatives offered points of value, although it must be said that the region's current problems are not the result of *unintended* incidents at sea. However, the apparent lack of coordination of proposals points to a weakness in the international response to China.

For all of the shared concern about the South China Sea on display at the Shangri-La Dialogue, it is also evident that the international community does feel constrained about how it should respond. For example, Kevin Andrews, the Australian defense minister, pointed out that more than half of Australian trade by volume transits the South China Sea and therefore "Australia urges all parties to exercise restraint, halt reclamation activities, refrain from provocative actions and take steps to ease tensions, because when tensions are high, the risk of miscalculation resulting in conflict is very real."[9] Andrews has since said Australian Defence Force ships and aircraft regularly transit the South China Sea and that a Chinese ADIZ would be ignored if one was declared over the region.[10] It does not

---

6. Lee Hsien Loong, Keynote Address, 14th IISS Asia Security Summit/Shangri-La Dialogue, May 29, 2015, https://www.iiss.org/en/events/shangri%20la%20dialogue/archive/shangri-la-dialogue-2015-862b/opening-remarks-and-keynote-address-6729/keynote-address-a51f.

7. Carter, "The United States and Challenges of Asia-Pacific Security."

8. Gen Nakatani, "New Forms of Security Collaboration in Asia," Remarks at the 14th IISS Asia Security Summit/Shangri-La Dialogue, Singapore, May 30, 2015, http://www.iiss.org/en/events/shangri%20la%20dialogue/archive/shangri-la-dialogue-2015-862b/plenary2-a5ab/nakatani-ecb0.

9. Kevin Andrews, "Global Security Challenges and the Asia-Pacific," Speech at the 14th IISS Asia Security Forum/Shangri-La Dialogue, Singapore, May 31, 2015, https://www.iiss.org/en/events/shangri%20la%20dialogue/archive/shangri-la-dialogue-2015-862b/plenary-5-8995/andrews-f56e.

10. David Wroe, "South China Sea: Australia Will Ignore Chinese Air Defence Zone, Says Kevin Andrews," *Sydney Morning Herald*, June 1, 2015, http://www.smh.com.au/federal-politics/political-news/south-china-sea-australia-will-ignore-chinese-air-defence-zone-says-kevin-andrews-20150601-ghe7o1.html#ixzz3gK8EUNmG.

seem that Australia has since sought to publicly exercise an overflight or passage of a naval vessel in areas close to Chinese island construction.

Prospects for More Concerted Action

What are the prospects for more concerted action on the part of the international community concerning China's assertive but opportunistic activities in the South China Sea? A broad assessment would council not raising undue expectations for more effective responses. Within ASEAN it is likely that there will continue to be calls for China to accede to a code of conduct on the South China Sea. However, ASEAN faces significant challenges to maintain or reinforce a unified approach on the issue. Consensus among the 10 member countries is difficult to achieve at the best of times and is made harder in this case because of the different perspectives brought to the table by claimant and non-claimant states. China has worked assiduously with some ASEAN states to encourage them not to stress the need for shared responses. Other ASEAN states face different preoccupations and challenges and are unlikely to drive the grouping to a more effective position. Indonesia in particular has taken an inward turn in policy and is unlikely, at least over the term of the Joko Widodo's presidency, to play a decisive regional leadership role in ASEAN unless there are major changes of personnel and/or a strategic jolt that forces Jakarta onto a different path.

Singapore's position is worth watching closely because it offers a lead indicator of assessments about ASEAN's prospects. Although Singapore continues to work hard within ASEAN, it is clear that the country's leadership feels a need to strengthen a wider range of connections beyond the organization. Thus Singapore continues to deepen defense cooperation with the United States, including to the point of providing low-key military support for coalition operations in the Middle East. Singapore also signed a comprehensive strategic partnership agreement with Australia on June 29, 2015, that will support a noticeably closer defense and intelligence relationship.[11] While the two countries have been long-term friends, it was not always the case that Singapore and Australia shared such close views on regional security priorities. In sum, Singapore is quietly positioning for a world in which ASEAN centrality in regional security is not an effective policy instrument.

ASEAN internal incapacity on the South China Sea complicates the positions of external interested players. India, for example, concerned with China's growing military presence in the Indian Ocean region, has clear interests in affirming the value of open sea lanes and airspace. But New Delhi will struggle for traction as an ASEAN dialogue partner in looking for tangible ways to demonstrate that interest in the South China Sea. As a second example, the European Union claims "a strategic interest in playing a fully-fledged role in and with Asia," including as a security partner willing to "step up its engagement with regional

11. Tony Abbott, "Joint Press Conference with Prime Minister Lee, Singapore," June 29, 2015, http://www.pm.gov.au/media/2015-06-29/joint-press-conference-prime-minister-lee-singapore.

security structures, fostering a rules-based approach to conflict management."[12] While this may lead to increased multilateral engagement with the ASEAN Regional Forum or the ASEAN Defense Ministers' Meeting Plus, this is unlikely to translate into a substantive military presence in the region that might, for example, seek to exercise free passage through the South China Sea.

Japan has a clear interest in diplomatically opposing China's maritime policies in the South China Sea and is looking to build support for its Shangri-La Dialogue Initiative on maritime confidence building. Japan's interest is clearly motivated by its own serious maritime sovereignty disputes with China. Tokyo has a strong U.S. alliance relationship; its highly capable Self-Defense Forces (SDF) underpins its policy objectives in the East China Sea. But although it is seeking to build more diplomatic leverage in Southeast Asia, it is unlikely to be able to take a lead role in regional consensus building.

The Five-Power Defence Arrangements (FPDA) linking Australia, Singapore, Malaysia, New Zealand, and the United Kingdom is Southeast Asia's only multilateral, operationally focused military grouping. In previous years it has undertaken military exercises in the South China Sea relating to its primary role of providing for the air defense of the Malay Peninsula. It is highly unlikely that the FPDA countries would have an interest in exercising a similar role that in any way challenged China's activities in the South China Sea. Singapore and Malaysia would most likely see such a possibility as too directly confrontational. New Zealand has previously declined to make any protest at China's establishment of the East China Sea ADIZ. Unlike other speakers at the 2015 Shangri-La Dialogue, the most forceful comment made by Gerry Brownlee, New Zealand's minister for defense, in Singapore was to say that "like other countries, New Zealand would be pleased to better understand the intentions of countries undertaking reclamation activities in those seas."[13] Wellington has already decided that its economic interests with China will trump strategic activism.

The United Kingdom struggles to sustain a substantive military presence in FPDA activities and Australia, at least at present, has a limited appetite for pushing the boundaries for high profile responses to China. Australia was one of a small number of countries that vocally protested China's declaration of an ADIZ over the East China Sea in late 2013, an act that earned Foreign Minister Julie Bishop a sharp televised rebuke from her Chinese counterpart, Wang Yi:

> The most important expectation that we have is that we need to respect each other's collective interests, accommodate any concerns and nurture a mutual trust. . . . In this area, I have to point out what Australia has said and done in terms

12. European External Action Service, "The European Union in a Changing Global Environment: A More Connected, Contested and Complex World," June 30, 2015, 13, http://eeas.europa.eu/docs/strategic_review/eu-strategic-review_strategic_review_en.pdf.

13. Gerry Brownlee, "Strengthening Regional Order in the Asia-Pacific," Remarks at the 14th IISS Asia Security Summit/Shangri-La Dialogue, Singapore, May 30, 2015, https://www.iiss.org/en/events/shangri%20la%20dialogue/archive/shangri-la-dialogue-2015-862b/plenary4-b8e3/brownlee-6d45.

> of the Air Defence Identification Zone in the East China Sea. That position has jeopardised that mutual trust . . . this is not what we desire to see.[14]

Since then there has been a lively debate in local media about the most effective way to frame Australia's position on the South China Sea. Former foreign minister Bob Carr is on-record advocating for a position of neutrality on China's claims vis-à-vis Japan and in other respects "emphasising the positive" in the Canberra-Beijing relationship.[15] At the other end of the spectrum, Secretary of Defence Dennis Richardson has dryly noted that China's island building is unlikely to be for promoting tourism: "given the size and modernisation of China's military, the use by China of land reclamation for military purposes would be of particular concern."[16] Thus far, however, Australian responses are significantly short of direct action to demonstrate the country's interests in free passage through the South China Sea.

These considerations suggest that the United States remains the key player with the greatest potential to galvanize a common response to China's activities in the South China Sea. On the positive side of the ledger, the United States continues to pursue closer military engagement with a large number of Asia-Pacific countries including Australia, New Zealand, the Philippines, Singapore, and Vietnam. This cooperation, along with existing alliance relationships, sustains an active and relevant U.S. strategic posture in the region. There is no doubt that Chinese assertiveness spurs a significant number of regional countries into closer engagement with the United States. Furthermore, U.S. political, diplomatic, and senior military engagement in the region, like Secretary Carter's Shangri-La Dialogue speech, makes a clear U.S. case for strong counter pressure against Chinese assertion in the South China Sea.

However, the U.S. strategic position has not stopped China from pursuing a more successfully assertive posture in the South and East China Seas for the last two years. Beijing calculates that nothing it has done so far has pushed Washington to the point where a direct confrontation establishes a red line that China cannot afford to cross. There is clearly much more at stake in the bilateral relationship than the South China Sea. Is it the case, as senior commentator Orville Schell recently argued in the *New York Times*, that the United States should acknowledge "that China is entitled to some kind of 'sphere of influence' in the South China Sea, just as the United States has in the Caribbean, without completely yielding to all of its territorial claims?"[17]

---

14. Scott Murdoch, "Angry China Rebukes Julie Bishop over East China Sea Dispute," *Australian*, December 7, 2013, http://www.theaustralian.com.au/national-affairs/foreign-affairs/angry-china-rebukes-julie-bishop-over-east-china-sea-dispute/story-fn59nm2j-1226777522342.

15. Peter Jennings, "Don't Fear What China May Think," *Australian*, July 13, 2015, http://www.theaustralian.com.au/opinion/dont-fear-what-china-may-think/story-e6frg6zo-1227439147922; Bob Carr, "Pragmatic with China," Letter to the Editor, *Australian*, July 14, 2015, http://www.theaustralian.com.au/opinion/letters/royal-commissions-task-is-to-find-and-expose-corruption/story-fn558imw-1227440376056.

16. Dennis Richardson, "Blamey Oration: The Strategic Outlook for the Indo-Pacific Region," Speech at the Royal United Services Institute's 3rd International Defence and Security Dialogue, *Sydney Morning Herald*, May 28, 2015, http://www.smh.com.au/national/defence-secretary-dennis-richardsons-blamey-oration-20150528-ghbf7w.html.

17. Orville Schell, "Can the U.S. and China Get Along?," *New York Times*, July 9, 2015, http://www.nytimes.com/2015/07/10/opinion/can-the-us-and-china-get-along.html?_r=0.

The problem with Schell's analogy is that the Caribbean is not surrounded by hotly competing great powers, nor does it act as the artery for a substantial proportion of global trade as does the South China Sea. The region is too contested and too economically important to treat as a Chinese lake. It remains the case that the United States is militarily distracted by the Middle East, uneasy about articulating red lines that may not be credible, concerned about bigger picture issues in the U.S.-China relationship, and has a second-term administration more focused on internal issues, but there is still a need to define a more coherent policy approach to the South China Sea. A strong policy approach that helps preserve a range of differing regional interests even without settling competing sovereignty claims would find a positive reception in the Asia Pacific.

Toward a Shared Strategy

This final section sets out a number of steps the United States and like-minded countries might act upon to develop a more effective shared strategy toward the South China Sea. Five immediate actions stand out as offering some promising steps forward.

1. The United States should open avenues for dialogue with Asia-Pacific countries and other parties with interests in the South China Sea. Most particularly this should include countries with substantial trading interests with China, like the Europeans and oil-producing Middle East countries, whose economic lifeline depends on unfettered access to the South China Sea. A Washington-initiated summit of countries with an interest in the South China Sea would help strengthen the consistency of government-to-government dialogue on the issue just as the Shangri-La Dialogue has done in Singapore. China would, of course, be a welcome participant, but the effect of this would be to demonstrate that more pluralist countries are better able to negotiate and share interests. A separate but aligned stream to this dialogue should be with the long standing Five-Eyes intelligence partners—Australia, Canada, New Zealand, the United Kingdom, and the United States—to ensure more aligned responses to evolving Chinese activities in the South China Sea.

2. A key point of discussion in Washington and with like-minded countries should be to anticipate responses that might be necessary to handle a Chinese announcement of an ADIZ across the South China Sea. The need is to learn from what was a poorly coordinated and unsustained reaction to the East China Sea ADIZ announcement in 2013. Beijing held back from an announcement of a new ADIZ before President Xi's September visit. But with the visit over and the United States beginning to focus on its presidential election campaign, it is possible that China might seek to take this next step aimed at consolidating its control of movement through the region. An ADIZ is incompatible with the objective of unfettered sea and air access through the region. Care must be taken to ensure that initial responses are not allowed to fade, giving way to de facto acceptance that China exercises a form of sovereign control over the region. It may be worth exploring the idea of declaring an international ADIZ, where ship and aircraft movements are pooled in a shared and openly

available platform for situational awareness. This would undercut any Chinese claim that it was necessary to operate its own ADIZ for operational reasons.

3. Washington and regional countries should take time to rethink the current language that is often deployed to respond to Chinese behavior. For example, calls for greater Chinese transparency in defense planning continue to be made long after the strategic purpose of gaining tight control in the South China Sea is readily apparent. China has long since learned to use the artifice of policy statements as a way to describe its actions. The idea of transparency has lost practical utility as a way of trying to force a more realistic discussion with China on its intentions.

   A key criterion here for nations with interests in the South China Sea must be to ensure that policy responses are appropriate to the most current Chinese action. For example, the emphasis on the legal basis (or lack thereof) of Chinese sovereignty claims seemed to be the core of many countries diplomatic talking points long after China had simply abandoned that argument in order to assert physical control over key features. Beijing benefited from allowing that discussion to meander on while sand was dredged and concrete poured.

4. Some degree of international coordination should take place to sustain a pattern of military overflights and freedom of navigation naval operations in the South China Sea, including within 12 nautical miles of disputed features. Two P-8 flights, no matter how welcome, do not serve to prove sustained international interest in the region.[18] In fact the opposite is true: if there are no follow-up flights from countries that claim strategic interests in the region, this only serves to show the relative absence of deep engagement in the security of the South China Sea. It follows that Australia, Japan, Singapore, EU countries, and others with a strategic interest in free access to the South China Sea need to exercise that interest in the form of actual overflights and freedom of navigation transits on the principle of "use it or lose it." What may be difficult to do today will only become harder in the future as a pattern of de facto Chinese control is established over the region.

Conclusion

This paper has argued that a mismatch of strategic motives and capabilities have made it possible for China to substantially assert its interests in the South China Sea while other interested parties have struggled to develop effective responses. China has adroitly taken advantage of a window of opportunity to assert control in some key areas at a point when other countries lacked the capacity or direct interest to intervene. The stakes, however, are rising because the strategic geography of the region—its criticality to seaborne trade and

18. The second of these P-8 flights, described as routine for U.S. operations in the South China Sea, took place on July 18, 2015, when Admiral Scott Swift, commander of the U.S. Pacific Fleet, undertook a seven-hour flight over the region. James Pearson and Ben Blanchard, "U.S. Admiral Says His South China Sea Surveillance Flight 'Routine,'" Reuters, July 20, 2015, http://www.reuters.com/article/2015/07/20/us-southchinasea-usa-idUSKCN0PU08720150720.

aircraft overflight—will ultimately force a more substantial counterresponse from countries with key interests at stake. It follows that there is a need for parties interested in the stability of the South China Sea to develop a more direct strategy to counter China's growing influence. As is so often the case, the United States is the essential player needed to galvanize a more coherent international reaction.

6 Some Legal Aspects of Current Developments in the South China Sea Dispute

Pham Lan Dung and Tran Huu Duy Minh

The South China Sea Dispute and Diplomatic Efforts by Parties

The dispute in the South China Sea, which involves six parties,[1] namely China, Brunei, Malaysia, the Philippines, Vietnam, and Taiwan (as an entity), is one of the world most complex disputes with overlapping claims relating to sovereignty over insular features and maritime claims. The complexity has been increased due to the fact that not all of the parties have clarified their positions on the legal regimes of features in the South China Sea.[2]

The uncertainty of which features may be rocks, entitled only to 12 nautical miles of territorial water or islands with full entitlement as a mainland under Article 121 of the United Nations Convention on the Law of the Sea (UNCLOS) or other features (submerged, low-tide elevation, reefs), in its turn, makes it difficult for the parties even to define the disputed area itself. In addition, the legal basis of the U-shaped (or nine-dash) line claim has never been clarified by China either in accordance with UNCLOS or under general international law. It remains uncertain whether the U-shape line is a line of claims to land, a line of historic title of China, or a line of national boundary.[3] This makes the area "a gray area of dispute" where the existence of dispute is undeniable, but its extent is not clear.

In the South China Sea dispute, parties are expected to settle their dispute through negotiation and consultation. The most prominent and tangible success was the adoption of

1. Indonesia is possibly also a party because the nine-dash line claimed by China overlaps the maritime claims of Indonesia. See I Made Andi Arsana and Clive Schofield, "Indonesia's 'Invisible' Border with China," in *Beijing's Power and China's Borders: Twenty Neighbors in Asia*, ed. Bruce A. Elleman, Stephen Kotkin, and Clive Schofield (Armonk, NY: M. E. Sharpe, 2013), 6162.

2. China officially published its U-shaped (nine-dash) line in 2009. Regarding the legal regime of maritime features, recently the Philippines clarified its position regarding the entitlement of several features in documents submitted in its arbitration case against China. China officially declared the entitlement of all islands in the Spratlys in Note Verbal CML/8/2011 to the United Nations Secretary General, April 14, 2011.

3. U.S. Department of State, "China: Maritime Claims in the South China Sea," *Limits in the Sea* 143 (December 5, 2014): 11–22, http://www.state.gov/documents/organization/234936.pdf.

the Declaration on the Conduct of Parties in the South China Sea (DOC) in 2002 between the Association of Southeast Asian Nations (ASEAN) and China. The DOC is a political instrument, thus technically has no legally binding effect. The DOC stipulates that "the Parties concerned undertake to resolve their territorial and jurisdictional disputes by peaceful means, without resorting to the threat or use of force, through friendly consultations and negotiations by sovereign states directly concerned, in accordance with universally recognized principles of international law, including the 1982 UN Convention on the Law of the Sea."[4]

The purpose of the DOC is to maintain the status quo of the dispute and facilitate cooperation between the parties. One of the core provisions stipulates that "the Parties undertake to self-refrain in conduct of activities that would complicate or escalate the dispute and affect peace and stability including among others, refraining from action of inhabiting on the presently uninhabited islands, reefs, shoals, cays, and other features."[5] Even though "inhabiting" is the only activity specified in the provision, the possibility of other activities that would complicate or escalate the dispute has been clearly stipulated in the provision.

The DOC has contributed to the management of the dispute, but recent tensions between the parties indicate that the DOC is not fully respected. There is lack of mutual understanding and political will to stabilize or settle the dispute. The positive development is that negotiations and consultations through diplomatic channels are ongoing; there is at least a willingness to discuss the dispute between the parties. The aim of these diplomatic efforts now is not to settle the dispute but to stabilize and manage it.

A code of conduct (COC) in the South China Sea is being negotiated between ASEAN members and China in order to develop a legal framework of general principles regulating the conduct of the parties in the South China Sea with the purpose of building trust and confidence, and preventing conflicts. The negotiation of the COC, however, has not yet achieved a significant outcome. The option of ASEAN member states concluding a COC between themselves with possible participation of non-ASEAN states, not limited to China only, has recently been discussed among scholars as an alternative to the conclusion of the COC with China.

Pending the adoption of the COC, it should be noted that China, in its position paper regarding arbitration with the Philippines,[6] has accepted the legal character of the DOC as a treaty. Clearly a DOC with legal effect was not the original intention of the parties, and, as a consequence, the language of the DOC is not legally binding.

4. Declaration on the Conduct of Parties in the South China Sea (DOC), Phnom Penh, November 4, 2002, Art. 4, http://www.asean.org/asean/external-relations/china/item/declaration-on-the-conduct-of-parties-in-the-south-china-sea.

5. Ibid., Art. 5.

6. China's Ministry of Foreign Affairs, "Position Paper of the Government of the People's Republic of China on the Matter of Jurisdiction in the South China Sea Arbitration Initiated by the Republic of the Philippines," December 7, 2014, para. 38, http://www.fmprc.gov.cn/mfa_eng/zxxx_662805/t1217147.shtml.

A question may be raised if ASEAN members would find it useful to agree to change the DOC from a political to a legal instrument and whether that would require the modification of the text of the DOC itself. China says, "Paragraph 4 of the DOC employs the term 'undertake,' which is also frequently used in international agreements to commit the parties to their obligations."[7] The term "undertake" is used in three other provisions of the DOC, including the above-mentioned Article 5 on self-restraint.

Besides the DOC and the COC, negotiations between the parties in the dispute have been conducted mainly in a bilateral manner with little information available. It is known that bilateral negotiations on maritime issues have been conducted between Vietnam and China and between China and the Philippines; it is unknown, however, if there is any such process between other parties.

Concerning negotiations between Vietnam and China, both parties have set up working groups on maritime delimitation in the area outside the closing line of the Tonkin Gulf and on joint development regarding less sensitive issues. There have been seven rounds of negotiations but the outcome is quite limited. Until now, there has been no progress regarding maritime delimitation in the areas outside the closing line of the Tonkin Gulf. The parties cannot reach an agreement on the overlapping area to be delimited. The reasons appear to be the sovereignty dispute over the Paracel Islands and the U-shaped line in the area.

On the issue of joint development, the differences between China and Vietnam remain large. However, in the latest round there was a small breakthrough and the parties reached a tentative agreement to conduct a joint survey in an area of 320 square kilometers (about 125 square miles), which is located right outside the closing line of Tonkin Gulf. The joint survey is expected to start this year.[8] This agreement is not a joint development project, but will serve as an information collecting step in preparation for further negotiations.

Recent Developments in the South China Sea Dispute

The ineffectiveness of the DOC is made evident by recent developments, such as the tension between China and the Philippines relating to the arbitration case initiated by Manila in 2013, the tension between China and Vietnam relating to the placement of the Haiyang Shiyou 981[9] oil rig by China in the exclusive economic zone (EEZ) and continental shelf of Vietnam, and most recently by the land reclamation and construction by China in the Spratly Islands. These developments are briefly analyzed below.

---

7. Ibid.

8. Joint Statement between Vietnam and China issued on the occasion of the visit of Nguyen Phu Trong, general secretary of the Communist Party of Vietnam to China, April 10, 2015.

9. "Hai Duong 981" in Vietnamese.

THE PHILIPPINES VERSUS CHINA ARBITRATION (2013)

This case was initiated against China by the Philippines in 2013 in accordance with the dispute settlement provisions in UNCLOS. China refused to appear before the arbitration tribunal at the Permanent Court of Arbitration. Despite refusing to appear, China released a position paper addressing the case on December 7, 2014, a week before the deadline for submission of a countermemorial set by the arbitration tribunal. Vietnam, as an interested third party, also submitted its position paper. In early July 2015 the first hearing concerning the jurisdiction of the arbitration tribunal was held.

The main requests by the Philippines are the legality of the U-shaped line claimed by China and the legal regime of several features in the South China Sea. The award may clarify one of the most disputed issues—the legal basis of the U-shaped line under UNCLOS. Moreover, the award may be considered a reference for parties to clarify the legal regime/entitlement of disputed features in the South China Sea.

UNCLOS also provides for optional exceptions for the jurisdiction of the forums. According to Article 298, states may excludes several types of disputes by a declaration, among others, including disputes concerning maritime delimitation or historic title.[10] China is the only party to make such a declaration in 2006. Moreover, as the UNCLOS dispute mechanism applies to disputes concerning the application or interpretation of UNCLOS, parties cannot utilize the mechanism to settle their territorial sovereignty disputes. Thus parties cannot resolve maritime delimitation disputes in the South China Sea if China is a party. However, it is still debated whether parties can bring disputes to an international court or tribunal if they prove that China has no lawful maritime claims.

In the case between the Philippines and China, the Philippines says clearly that all of its requests are not concerning territorial sovereignty or maritime delimitation. It only requests the arbitration to adjudicate the legal basis of the U-shaped line and the legal regime of several features notwithstanding who has sovereignty over these features.

In response China has three arguments to prove that the requests by the Philippines are concerning maritime delimitation, which was excluded by the 2006 declaration in accordance with Article 298. First, China argues that the "legal issues as those presented by the Philippines in the present arbitration, including maritime claims, the legal nature of maritime features, the extent of relevant maritime rights, and law enforcement activities at sea, are all fundamental issues dealt with in past cases of maritime delimitation decided by international judicial or arbitral bodies and in State practice concerning maritime delimitation."[11]

China argues that the maritime delimitation involves that application of UNCLOS, general international law, and other factors to reach an equitable solution, and that the

10. UN Convention on the Law of the Sea (UNCLOS), December 10, 1982, Art. 298, http://www.un.org/Depts/los/convention_agreements/texts/unclos/closindx.htm.

11. China's Ministry of Foreign Affairs, "Position Paper," para. 66.

decision sought by the Philippines may destroy the integrity and indivisibility of maritime delimitation. In its last argument China says that some of the requests of the Philippines, such as the request that China has unlawfully interfered with the enjoyment and exercise by the Philippines of sovereign rights in its EEZ and continental shelf, are obviously an attempt to seek recognition of Philippine rights over particular areas, and thus are actually a maritime delimitation case.

It is true that some minor requests by the Philippines are formulated in a way that could be considered to be concerning maritime delimitation. However, this might be done intentionally in order to emphasize the contrast between these requests and the main requests, which have not been related to either sovereignty or delimitation. The requests to clarify the legal basis of the U-shaped line and legal regime of several features are not intended to delimit maritime areas between states. The Philippines is just asking what can be claimed by states in the South China Sea in accordance with UNCLOS. Maritime delimitation can only exist if there is an overlapping area between lawful claims by states; a state cannot insist to delimit maritime areas with other states if it has no lawful maritime claims. Thus the issue of lawfulness of claims is a predelimitation issue.

It is expected that the arbitration tribunal will decide that it has jurisdiction over the issue of the legal regime of features in the South China Sea, the question that has never been addressed directly by any tribunal in previous jurisprudence. It is still unclear whether the arbitration tribunal will reformulate the question asked by the Philippines or will address it in its initial form.

As related to the legal basis of the U-shape line, if the arbitration tribunal, for any reason, does not find that it has jurisdiction, this should be for the reason that the U-shape line claim has been too vague and has never been clarified by China and hence cannot be considered as an existing claim but rather in its early-formation stage. In addition, the best the arbitration tribunal can do in its reasoning is to clarify that the U-shape line claim, in whichever possible form, has no legal ground either under UNCLOS or under general international law.

THE OIL RIG INCIDENT (2014)

From May to July 2014 China and Vietnam faced diplomatic tensions related to the employment of the Haiyang Shiyou 981 oil rig by China in the area between the Vietnamese coast and the Paracel Islands, whose sovereignty are disputed by the two states. The location of the oil rig was about 20 nautical miles from the nearest feature in the Paracels and 130 nautical miles from the coast of Vietnam.

Beijing argued that China has sovereignty over the Paracel Islands and that the oil rig was "conducting normal activities" in the waters of the Paracel Islands. It is interesting that although the location of the oil rig is within the 200-nautical-mile entitlement of the EEZ and continental shelf of Hainan Island (China), China never referred to the island in its official statements.[12] By ignoring Hainan Island, one may infer that China wanted to realize its claims for 200-nautical-mile maritime zones for the Paracel Islands and its U-shaped line.

Vietnam, on the other hand, reaffirmed its sovereignty over the Paracel Islands and claimed that the oil rig was within the EEZ and continental shelf from the Vietnamese coast. This may be understood that Vietnam implicitly recognizes that features in the Paracel Islands can only be considered as "rocks" provided under Article 121(3) of the UNCLOS, thus they only have a 12-nautical-mile territorial sea.

Putting aside the Paracel Islands, the oil rig was placed in the overlapping area of EEZ and continental shelf generating from the Hainan Island and the coast of Vietnam. In such area, states have an obligation to enter into provisional arrangements and not to jeopardize or hamper the reaching of a final agreement under Article 74(3) and 83(3) of UNCLOS. In the case between Guyana and Suriname, the Permanent Court of Arbitration's tribunal placed emphasis on the phrase "in a spirit of understanding and cooperation" and held that any unilateral activity that might affect the other party's rights in a permanent manner or lead to a permanent physical change, such as exploitation of oil and gas reserves, would be prohibited.[13] The placement of the oil rig without prior notification demonstrates a clear disregard for a spirit of understanding or cooperation. Moreover, as China had never previously conducted any oil-related activities in this area, the placement of the oil rig changed the status quo of the area and was violating its obligation to refrain from complicating and escalating the dispute under the DOC.

LAND RECLAMATION AND CONSTRUCTION ACTIVITIES IN THE SPRATLY ISLANDS

Around the time of the oil rig incident with Vietnam, China also started land reclamation and construction activities in several features in the Spratly Islands. Other parties to the dispute have been active for years, but not in the massive scale that China is pursuing. The total area of land reclamation and construction has not been calculated yet, but the figure for two of the seven features concerned is about 3.6 square miles as of June 16, 2015.[14]

Ashton Carter, U.S. secretary of defense, said, "China has reclaimed over 2,000 acres, more than all other claimants combined . . . and more than in the entire history of the region. And China did so in only the last 18 months. It is unclear how much farther China will go."[15] According to the U.S. Department of State, the total area is nearly four times that

12. Pham Lan Dung, "Some Legal Aspects of the Drilling Rig Incident in the South China Sea in 2014," Japan Institute of International Affairs, June 30, 2015, http://www2.jiia.or.jp/pdf/fellow_report/150630_Ms_Dung_oil_rig.pdf.

13. Guyana vs. Suriname, Permanent Court of Arbitration, Award, September 17, 2007, http://www.pca-cpa.org/Guyana-Suriname%20Award70f6.pdf?fil_id=664.

14. Asia Maritime Transparency Initiative, "Diplomacy Changes, Construction Continues: New Images of Mischief and Subi Reefs," CSIS, June 18, 2015, http://amti.csis.org/diplomacy-changes-construction-continues-new-images-of-mischief-and-subi-reefs/.

15. Ashton Carter, "A Regional Security Architecture Where Everyone Rises," Speech at the 14th IISS [International Institute for Strategic Studies] Asia Security Summit/Shangri-La Dialogue, Singapore, May 30, 2015, http://www.defense.gov/News/Speeches/Article/606676.

of the other five parties combined and China is building a landing strip—the longest in the Spratly Islands.[16] Other parties, especially Vietnam and the Philippines, have strongly objected to these activities. ASEAN has expressed concern about Chinese land reclamation and said that the activity "has eroded trust and confidence and may undermine peace, security and stability in the South China Sea."[17]

According to the DOC, parties to the dispute "undertake to exercise self-restraint in the conduct of activities that would complicate or escalate disputes and affect peace and stability including, among others, refraining from action of inhabiting on the presently uninhabited islands, reefs, shoals, cays, and other features and to handle their differences in a constructive manner."[18] It is clear that the massive land reclamation and construction activities by China have caused tensions and have escalated disputes, because it changed the status quo of the dispute.

Another aspect of China's reclamation activities is whether the changes in the characteristics of those features will affect the legal regime under UNCLOS. Under the provisions of UNCLOS, it can be inferred that the legal regime of a particular feature may not be affected by artificial activities because the regime of that feature is established on the basis of its natural conditions. Thus the land reclamation and construction activities by China or other parties may not have any effect on the regime of original features.

Captain J. Ashley Roach, a retired U.S. Navy judge advocate, argues that China's land reclamation and construction demonstrate not only noncompliance with the DOC but also noncompliance with international environmental law and might affect the Philippines-China arbitration case.[19] He also emphasizes that China's activities cannot change the legal status of the features and that other countries should object (in the form of declarations and actions).

POSSIBLE NEXT TENSION: AIR DEFENSE IDENTIFICATION ZONE (ADIZ)

Some security experts suggest that the land reclamation and construction activities by China are the first step to prepare the infrastructure for the establishment of an ADIZ in the South China Sea. The reclaimed features could be the base for an airport and would extend the reach of the Chinese air force to the south of the South China Sea.

The establishment of ADIZs is neither prohibited nor explicitly permitted by international law. Canada, the United States, Japan, Korea, and others established ADIZs in the past. In 2013 China established an ADIZ in the East China Sea, which covered a large

16. Daniel R. Russel, "Maritime Issues in East Asia," Testimony before the Senate Foreign Relations Committee, Washington, DC, May 13, 2015, http://www.state.gov/p/eap/rls/rm/2015/05/242262.htm.

17. Chairman's Statement of the 26th ASEAN Summit, Kuala Lumpur and Langkawi, Malaysia, April 27, 2015, para. 59, http://www.asean.org/news/asean-statement-communiques/item/chairman-s-statement-of-the-26th-asean-summit.

18. DOC, Art. 5.

19. Ashley Roach, "China's Shifting Sands in the Spratlys," *ASIL Insights* 19, no. 15 (July 15, 2015), http://www.asil.org/insights/volume/19/issue/15/chinas-shifting-sands-spratlys.

airspace beyond the territorial sea of China, including the airspace over Senkaku/Diaoyu Islands disputed with Japan. China requires all airplanes (commercial or governmental) to submit information even when they are not headed to or departing from a Chinese airport or entering into Chinese airspace.[20]

Several states, including the United States and Japan, objected to the declaration of the East China Sea ADIZ by China. Robert Beckman and Hao Duy Phan analyze the reasons behind these objections, including that the ADIZ applies even to aircraft that do no plan to enter China's national airspace, it covers the disputed Senkaku/Diaoyu Islands, and it applies to military aircraft.[21]

The situation in the South China Sea is more complex than in the East China Sea. The ADIZ in the East China Sea only covers a small group of disputed islands. But in the South China Sea, the disputed islands are much greater in number and scattered across a much larger area. The sovereignty disputes over hundreds of features make the legal regime over them disputed as well. A state cannot establish an ADIZ over the airspace of other states until the dispute is settled. The establishment of an ADIZ would escalate the South China Sea dispute in violation of the DOC. Beckman and Hao argue that if an ADIZ is established over the Paracel Islands, Scarborough Shoal, or the Spratly Islands, it could be considered provocative or aggressive and would complicate the dispute and worsen relations between China and other states in the region.[22]

UNCLOS Dispute Settlement Mechanism and the South China Sea Dispute

In the South China Sea dispute, even though diplomatic means have been more preferable than judicial means, there are some signs that the use of third-party mechanisms, including judicial, is not excluded.[23] In the case between the Philippines and China, it is observed that due to the lack of goodwill from China, there have been tensions between the two sides. China repeatedly refuses to accept the arbitration suit and emphasizes that the dispute can only be settled by negotiations and through consultations between the parties directly concerned. In the oil rig incident, Vietnam declared that it would use all peaceful means to

---

20. Matthew Waxman, "China's ADIZ at One Year: International Legal Issues," Asia Maritime Transparency Initiative, CSIS, November 25, 2014, http://amti.csis.org/chinas-adiz-at-one-year-international-legal-issues/.

21. Robert Beckman and Hao Duy Phan, "Air Defence Identification Zones: Implications for Freedom of Overflight and Maritime Disputes" (paper presented at the International Workshop on The South China Sea: Cooperation for Regional Security and Development, Danang, Vietnam, November 2014).

22. Ibid.

23. There were disputes concerning states in the region settled by international courts or tribunals in the past such as the sovereignty disputes between Cambodia and Thailand (International Court of Justice [ICJ] judgment, 1962), Malaysia and Singapore (ICJ judgment, 2008), Indonesia and Malaysia (ICJ judgment, 2001), and the maritime delimitation dispute between Myanmar and Bangladesh (International Tribunal for the Law of the Sea [ITLOS] judgment, 2012). These cases indicate that those states at least considered a third-party mechanism as a possible solution.

settle the dispute in accordance with international law, [24] not excluding the judicial means.[25]

The jurisdiction of international courts or tribunals is based on mutual consent between parties; it is a well-established principle that a state cannot be brought before an international court or tribunal without its consent. Looking into the South China Sea dispute there is no consent between all of the parties, except the compulsory dispute settlement of UNCLOS. By becoming parties to UNCLOS, states agree in advance that they accept the jurisdiction of the four judicial forums to settle their dispute concerning the application or interpretation of UNCLOS: the International Tribunal for the Law of the Sea (ITLOS), the International Court of Justice (ICJ), arbitration under Annex VII, and arbitration under Annex VIII. Thus, parties may bring a case against other parties at any time, provided that the conditions under UNCLOS are met.

UTILIZING THE MECHANISM TO CLARIFY THE CONTENT AND EXTENT OF DISPUTES

It seems obvious that if parties to the dispute clarify their claims and the legal basis of these claims that future tensions could be limited. When the content and scope of the dispute are clear, the parties will be aware of their rights and obligations. Any party or some parties may voluntarily clarify their claims. They may use judicial means to do this by, for example, utilizing the UNCLOS dispute settlement mechanism in the Philippines versus China case. If the award positively responds to the requests by the Philippines, the content and extent of the dispute will be significantly clarified, paving the way for ultimate settlement in accordance with international law.

There is another way to clarify the dispute by advisory proceedings before ITLOS. The tribunal allows states to conclude an agreement giving it advisory jurisdiction to address a legal question. Article 138 of the Rules of the Tribunal provides that "the Tribunal may give an advisory opinion on a legal question if an international agreement related to the purposes of the Convention specifically provides for the submission to the Tribunal of a request for such an opinion."[26]

There had been debates on the legal basis of the tribunal's advisory jurisdiction, but the tribunal has confirmed its jurisdiction and given its first advisory opinion in Case No. 21. Accordingly, for the tribunal to have advisory jurisdiction, the ASEAN states have to conclude an international agreement relating to the purpose of UNCLOS, authorizing a body to make a request for an advisory opinion from ITLOS on the lawfulness and extent of claims in

---

24. The policy of resorting to all peaceful measures to settle the disputes in the South China Sea has been reiterated by Le Hai Bi, Vietnam's Ministry of Foreign Affairs spokesperson. See, for example, see the press briefing by Binh on May 15, 2014, http://www.mofa.gov.vn/en/tt_baochi/pbnfn/ns140516233943.

25. Nguyen Thi Thanh Ha, director of the Department of International Law and Treaties, Ministry of Foreign Affairs of Vietnam, in a press conference on developments in South China Sea on May 23, 2014, said, "The use of peaceful means including international tribunals is in conformity with international law."

26. International Tribunal for the Law of the Sea, Rules of the Tribunal (ITLOS/8), amended March 17, 2009, Art. 138, https://www.itlos.org/fileadmin/itlos/documents/basic_texts/Itlos_8_E_17_03_09.pdf.

accordance with the convention. ASEAN members may sign an agreement to submit a request to ITLOS to give advisory opinion. The act may be done by two or more parties to the dispute.

UTILIZING THE MECHANISM TO SETTLE DISPUTES IN OVERLAPPING AREAS

Another suggestion is that, in the overlapping areas generating from lawful claims, parties consider initiating judicial proceedings before international courts or tribunals under UNCLOS to settle incidents between them. In such a case UNCLOS imposes obligations under Article 74(3) and 83(3): "Pending agreement as provided for in paragraph 1, the States concerned, in a spirit of understanding and cooperation, shall make every effort to enter into provisional arrangements of a practical nature and, during this transitional period, not to jeopardize or hamper the reaching of the final agreement. Such arrangements shall be without prejudice to the final delimitation."[27] These provisions establish a legal regime for overlapping areas.

For example, in the Haiyang Shiyou 981 incident, the placement of the oil rig was in the overlapping area of EEZ and continental shelf generating from Hainan Island and the coast of Vietnam notwithstanding China's U-shaped line. Vietnam could request the arbitration tribunal to declare that by placing and drilling in the area China had violated its obligations under Article 74(3) and 83(3).

However, the main obstacle lies in the 2006 declaration by China in accordance with Article 298. The declaration excludes maritime delimitation concerning Article 74 and 83, which is entitled "Delimitation of the exclusive economic zone/continental shelf between States with opposite or adjacent coasts." One may argue that because Article 298 refers to Article 74 and 83 it covers paragraph 3 as well. Thus the obligations in the overlapping areas cannot be revoked before international tribunals or courts.

On the other hand, one could argue that Article 298 refers to maritime delimitation under Article 74 and 83 and does not cover issues *before* delimitation. Paragraph 3 of both articles is concerning cooperation between parties pending delimitation.[28] Thus it means that cooperation may be distinct from the process of maritime delimitation. The cooperation, for instance in the form of provisional arrangements, may or may not be part of maritime delimitation. The authors believe that the second line of argument should be upheld.

On a case-by-case basis, international tribunals will have to decide whether paragraph 3 of Articles 74 and 83 concerns maritime delimitation or a predelimitation obligation. In the Haiyang Shiyou 981 incident, it is hard to argue that the placement of an oil rig in the overlapping area is related to the issue of maritime delimitation. Moreover, if the first line of argument is upheld, international courts or tribunals cannot contribute to the fulfillment of the purposes of UNCLOS: to promote peaceful uses of seas and oceans.[29]

27. UNCLOS, Art. 74(3) and 83(3).
28. Pham Lan Dung, "Some Legal Aspects of the Drilling Rig Incident."
29. UNCLOS, Preamble.

7 | The Regional Military and Paramilitary Balance

The Widening Chasm between China and Southeast Asia

Ian Storey

The gap that existed two decades ago between the military power of the People's Republic of China (PRC) and the countries of Southeast Asia has widened into a chasm. According to one estimate, in 2014 China's defense outlay was $216 billion—the second largest in the world, the largest in Asia, and six times bigger than the combined defense budgets of the 10 countries that make up the Association of Southeast Asian Nations (ASEAN).[1]

China's leaders have determined to transform the country into a global maritime power, and to that end the People's Liberation Army Navy (PLAN) is emerging as Asia's largest and most capable navy. China is also rapidly expanding its coast guard and using it as the lead agency to advance its territorial and maritime jurisdictional claims in the South and East China Seas. The ongoing reclamation projects in the Spratly Islands will enable China to project decisive power into the very heart of maritime Southeast Asia with the ultimate goal of achieving dominance within the so-called nine-dash line.

While Southeast Asian countries have ramped up their defense budgets over the past few years, and acquired new, larger, and more lethal assets, their navies, and especially their coast guards, are dwarfed by China's. Neither individually nor collectively can the countries of Southeast Asia match China's growing military power. Instead they continue to put their faith in talks with China to mitigate tensions in the South China Sea, even as that process looks increasingly irrelevant, and to rely on the United States and others to balance China, even as that strategy has the potential to create invidious dilemmas for them in an era of growing Sino-U.S. competition in Southeast Asia.

1. Sam Perlo-Freeman, Aude Fleurant, Pieter D. Wezeman, and Siemon T. Wezeman, "Trends in World Military Expenditure, 2014," SIPRI Fact Sheet, April 2015, http://books.sipri.org/files/FS/SIPRIFS1504.pdf.

China's Military/Paramilitary Modernization Continues Apace

Since the beginning of 2015, a series of reports have been published examining China's evolving defense policy and the rapid modernization of its military and paramilitary forces.[2] Overall, these reports contain few real surprises. Instead they underscore a phenomenon that has been apparent for more than a decade: China's emergence as Asia's paramount military power and the ever widening gap between the size and capabilities of the People's Liberation Army (PLA) and those of its neighbors, particularly in Southeast Asia where Beijing is in dispute with four countries—Vietnam, the Philippines, Malaysia, and Brunei—over the sovereignty of several island groups and maritime boundaries.

In 2015 Chinese defense spending did not increase as much as in the past few years, but it still outpaced gross domestic product (GDP) growth: 10 percent versus 7 percent.[3] Estimates of China's defense outlay vary considerably. The U.S. Department of Defense (DOD), for instance, assesses China's "total military spending" at $165 billion, while the Stockholm International Peace Institute (SIPRI) estimates the real figure to be closer to $216 billion.[4] Chinese official figures put defense spending at approximately $145 billion (around only 2 percent of the country's GDP). This positions China as the world's second largest defense spender (behind America's still gargantuan outlay of $610 billion) and by far the biggest in Asia. Based on SIPRI figures, in 2014 China accounted for 52.6 percent of defense spending in Northeast, Southeast, and South Asia ($216 billion of $411 billion) and had a defense budget that was greater than all 23 countries in those three regions combined.[5]

Although China does not release budgetary allocations for each service, it is apparent that the PLAN has been a key beneficiary of the country's growing defense budget. This is unsurprising. Since the end of the last decade, the Chinese Communist Party's top leaders have declared their determination to transform China into a global maritime power, and that the accomplishment of that goal is a vital prerequisite for it to achieve great power—perhaps even superpower—status. Indeed, China's 2015 defense white paper called for

2. See, for example, Ministry of National Defense, *China's Military Strategy* (Beijing: State Council Information Office, May 2015), http://news.usni.org/2015/05/26/document-chinas-military-strategy; Office of the Secretary of Defense, *Military and Security Developments Involving the People's Republic of China 2015: Annual Report to Congress* (Washington, DC: Department of Defense, April 7, 2015), http://www.defense.gov/Portals/1/Documents/pubs/2015_China_Military_Power_Report.pdf; Office of Naval Intelligence, *The PLA Navy: New Capabilities and Missions for the 21st Century* (Washington, DC: Office of Naval Intelligence, 2015), http://www.oni.navy.mil/Intelligence_Community/china_media/2015_PLA_NAVY_PUB_Print_Low_Res.pdf; Ronald O'Rourke, *China Naval Modernization: Implications for U.S. Navy Capabilities—Background and Issues for Congress* (Washington, DC: Congressional Research Service, September 2015), https://www.fas.org/sgp/crs/row/RL33153.pdf.

3. "China raises defence budget by 10.1%, the slowest growth in military spending in 5 years," *Straits Times*, March 5, 2015, http://www.straitstimes.com/asia/east-asia/china-raises-defence-budget-by-101-the-slowest-growth-in-military-spending-in-5-years.

4. Perlo-Freeman et al., "Trends in World Military Expenditure 2014."

5. Stockholm International Peace Research Institute (SIPRI), "SIPRI Military Expenditure Database," accessed August 28, 2015, http://www.sipri.org/research/armaments/milex/milex_database.

nothing less than a fundamental change in the national mindset, away from a traditional focus on the land to one that emphasizes the sea.[6]

As most analysts seem to agree, China's armed forces continue to suffer from important shortcomings, especially when it comes to institutional and combat capabilities.[7] According to the DOD, overall the PLA is increasingly "able to project power to assert regional dominance during peacetime and contest U.S. military superiority during a regional conflict."[8] The PLAN in particular has improved training, leadership, and operational efficiency, and while the aggregate size of the fleet has fallen slightly, it has increased the capabilities of its platforms by commissioning larger and more sophisticated multirole assets.[9] China's navy is quickly "assuming its place among the most powerful navies in Asia."[10]

Those who have assessed China's overall maritime military capabilities have included the Chinese coast guard, which has greatly expanded over the past few years and which has been aptly described by U.S. Naval War College professor Andrew Erickson as "China's Second Navy."[11] As tensions in the South and East China Seas have risen over the past few years, China has used the coast guard as its lead agency to respond to perceived provocations by the other disputants as well as to advance its territorial and maritime jurisdictional claims, largely because white hulls appear less confrontational than gray hulls.

But while the coast guard takes the lead, the PLAN is never far behind. It stands ready to intervene and provide support if necessary. Following the consolidation of China's civilian maritime law enforcement agencies, the coast guard and navy have begun acting in a more coordinated manner. PLAN/coast guard coordination has been apparent in all of China's most recent high-profile maritime standoffs, including around the Senkaku/Diaoyu Islands since 2012, at Scarborough Shoal in 2012, Second Thomas Reef in 2014 (when Chinese vessels tried to prevent the Philippines from resupplying military personnel on the atoll) and during the Sino-Vietnamese crisis triggered by Beijing's deployment of the massive Haiyang Shiyou 981 oil rig into Vietnam's claimed 200-nautical-mile exclusive economic zone (EEZ) in May–June 2014.

China's strategy has been dubbed by some analysts as China's "cabbage strategy" and by the U.S. Defense Department as "low-intensity coercion."[12] The expansion of the coast guard has been rapid: 50 oceangoing patrol boats have been added since 2004, and the U.S. Defense Department estimates another 100 of various sizes will be added in the coming

6. Ministry of National Defense, *China's Military Strategy*.

7. See, for instance, Wendell Minnick, "Report: China's Incomplete Transformation," *Defense News*, February 11, 2015; Dennis Blasko, "Ten Reasons Why China Will Have Trouble Fighting a Modern War," *War on the Rocks*, February 18, 2015, http://warontherocks.com/2015/02/ten-reasons-why-china-will-have-trouble-fighting-a-modern-war/.

8. Office of the Secretary of Defense, *Military and Security Developments*, 43.

9. Office of Naval Intelligence, *The PLA Navy*, 4.

10. Ibid., 10.

11. Andrew S. Erickson, "How U.S. Navy Intelligence Sees China's Maritime Forces," *War on the Rocks*, April 10, 2015, http://warontherocks.com/2015/04/how-u-s-navy-intel-sees-chinas-maritime-forces/.

12. Office of the Secretary of Defense, *Military and Security Developments*, 3.

years, increasing total force levels by 25 percent.[13] Together with more than 300 PLAN surface ships, submarines, patrol vessels, and amphibious landing ships, China today is able to field an impressive maritime force, second only to the United States.

While contingencies in the Taiwan Strait remain the central driver of China's defense modernization program, the naval and air assets that China has acquired to retake Taiwan by force can also be used to secure Beijing's expansive maritime claims in the South China Sea.[14] Since late 2013 China has embarked on an impressive project that will ultimately allow it to project military power into the very heart of maritime Southeast Asia in pursuit of those claims—the transformation of seven features in the Spratlys (Fiery Cross Reef, South Johnson Reef, Hughes Reef, Gaven Reef, Mischief Reef, Subi Reef, and Cuarteron Reef) into large, manmade islands on which it is currently developing extensive military and civilian infrastructure including harbors, multistory buildings, radar and surveillance facilities, helipads, and two airstrips.[15]

China has brushed off international criticism of the reclamations by arguing that it is acting within its sovereign rights and that in any case it is only doing what some of the other claimants have been doing on their atolls over the past few decades. Chinese officials have also stressed that the facilities on the artificial islands are designed *primarily* for civilian use and that they will help provide public goods such as search and rescue support, meteorological services, and scientific research.[16] Such claims have been met with skepticism, especially by China's neighbors.

In reality, it is clear that the main purpose of the reclaimed atolls is strategic. The harbors and other facilities under construction will enable the PLAN and coast guard to maintain a permanent presence in and around the Spratlys, without the need to return to mainland ports for reprovisioning, maintenance, and crew rotation. Forward deployed PLAN and coast guard vessels can be used to enforce Beijing's sovereignty and sovereign rights claims in the South China Sea, and to provide protection for Chinese fishing vessels and drilling platforms operating in the EEZs of other coastal states that are within China's so-called nine-dash line.

PLAN and coast guard assets may also be used to increase pressure on the other claimants to vacate the atolls under their control. Radar, surveillance, and communication systems, together with the presence of fighter jets operating from airfields on Fiery Cross and Subi Reefs, will also enable China to greatly enhance its maritime domain awareness in the South China Sea. Perhaps sooner rather than later China will declare an air defense identification zone (ADIZ) over the Spratlys to underscore its jurisdictional claims, as it controversially did over parts of the East China Sea in 2013.

---

13. Ibid., 44.
14. Office of Naval Intelligence, *The PLA Navy*, 8.
15. This sections draws on Ian Storey, "China's Terraforming in the Spratlys: A Game Changer in the South China Sea?," *ISEAS Perspective* 29 (June 23, 2015).
16. Ministry of Foreign Affairs, "Foreign Ministry Spokesperson Hua Chunying's Regular Press Conference on April 9, 2015," http://www.fmprc.gov.cn/mfa_eng/xwfw_665399/s2510_665401/t1253488.shtml.

Despite China's attempt to put a civilian gloss on the reclamations, they are overwhelmingly strategic in purpose. They will almost certainly exacerbate tensions with the other claimants—especially the Philippines and Vietnam—as well as the United States. We can expect to see more skirmishes at sea, and in the air, involving patrol boats, warships, fishing boats, survey ships, and surveillance aircraft when the Chinese facilities on the seven features are up and running.

The Balance of Power between China and Southeast Asia: Too Late to Mind the Gap

China, of course, has not been the only country in Asia to have ramped up its defense spending. According to SIPRI, defense spending in Southeast Asia rose by 5 percent between 2012 and 2013, higher than in East Asia (4.7 percent) and Asia and Oceania as a whole (3.6 percent).[17]

Between 2010 and 2014, all the Southeast Asian claimants increased defense spending: Vietnam by 59.1 percent, the Philippines 35 percent, Malaysia 27.6 percent, and Brunei 35 percent. Non-claimant countries also bolstered their defense budgets: Indonesia by 50.6 percent, Singapore 21.4 percent, and Thailand 15.5 percent. Across the whole region, the average increase was 37.6 percent.[18]

Certainly in the cases of Vietnam and the Philippines—and to a lesser extent Malaysia and Brunei—the South China Sea dispute has been an important factor in driving up defense budgets. It has also been a factor for other countries around the region, including Indonesia and Singapore, that have important economic and strategic interests in the South China Sea.

Southeast Asian navies have used the increase in defense dollars to purchase some impressive capabilities. Regional countries are equipping themselves with larger, longer range, and better armed warships—though offshore patrol vessels, corvettes, and frigates rather than destroyers—and vessels equipped for expeditionary warfare.[19]

Most importantly, perhaps, Southeast Asian navies have acquired, or expanded, their subsurface capabilities. Singapore now has six refurbished submarines from Sweden and has ordered two new vessels from Germany. Malaysia operates two French-designed submarines. Vietnam has taken delivery of four *Kilo*-class submarines from Russia and will receive two more soon. Indonesia has ordered three submarines from South Korea. Thailand recently announced it was buying three submarines from China.

---

17. Sam Perlo-Freeman and Carina Solmirano, "Trends in World Military Expenditure, 2013," SIPRI Fact Sheet, April 2014, http://books.sipri.org/files/FS/SIPRIFS1404.pdf.

18. Zachary Abuza, "Analyzing Southeast Asia's Military Expenditures," *CogitAsia*, May 7, 2015, http://cogitasia.com/analyzing-southeast-asias-military-expenditures/.

19. Richard Bitzinger, "South-East Asia Naval Expansion and Its Risks," *Straits Times*, May 14, 2015, http://www.straitstimes.com/opinion/south-east-asia-naval-expansion-and-its-risks.

According to defense analyst Richard Bitzinger, Southeast Asian naval acquisitions over the past decade amount to more than the mere replacement of obsolete vessels: "Local navies are acquiring greater lethality and accuracy at longer ranges" as well as "new or increased capabilities for force projection, operational manoeuvres, and speed."[20] And Southeast Asia's "arms dynamic" looks set to continue: IHS Jane's projects Southeast Asian defense spending will rise to $52 billion in 2012 from $42 billion in 2015.[21]

Southeast Asian states are also building their coast guards, though increases in spending and acquisitions remain far below that of their naval counterparts.[22] Because they will always remain the poor cousin to regional navies, and yet increasingly at the sharp end of maritime disputes with China, regional coast guards are being provided ships, equipment, and training by external powers with a vested interest in maintaining the status quo and worried by rising tensions in the South China Sea.

Japan has taken the lead, and pledged to provide the Philippine coast guard with 10 patrol vessels and Vietnam's civilian maritime agency with four. The United States is also committed to improving the maritime security capabilities of Southeast Asian navies and coast guards. In May 2015 at the Shangri-La Dialogue in Singapore, Ashton Carter, the U.S. secretary of defense, announced the establishment of a $425 million Southeast Asia maritime security initiative to fund capacity-building support across the region.[23] In Vietnam, where he visited immediately following Singapore, Carter revealed that $18 million would be provided to Vietnam to buy U.S.-built patrol boats.[24]

Despite increases in defense spending and the acquisition of new capabilities, by almost every measure Southeast Asia's military power is dwarfed by that of China's. In 2000 China's $22.2 billion defense budget was only slightly higher than the 10 ASEAN members, who collectively spent $19.55 billion. By 2014 Southeast Asian defense spending had risen to $38.2 billion—but at $216.37 billion, China's defense outlay was almost six times larger.[25]

A comparison of the number of naval and coast guard vessels China and the ASEAN states possess is problematic, not least because aggregate figures do not indicate relative capabilities. Nevertheless, the figures are quite striking. The U.S. Defense Department estimates that in 2014 the PLAN's order of battle included 56 submarines, 1 aircraft carrier,

20. Ibid.

21. Siva Govindasamy, "South China Sea Dispute: Southeast Asia Maritime Build-Up Accelerates," *Sydney Morning Herald*, May 26, 2015, http://www.smh.com.au/world/south-china-sea-dispute-southeast-asia-maritime-buildup-accelerates-20150525-gh9j7q.html.

22. Richard Bitzinger, "Coast Guards in the South China Sea: Proxy Fighters?," *RSIS Commentary*, no. 121 (May 20, 2015), https://www.rsis.edu.sg/wp-content/uploads/2015/05/CO15121.pdf.

23. Ashton Carter, "The United States and Challenges of Asia-Pacific Security," Speech at the 14th IISS [International Institute for Strategic Studies] Asia Security Summit/Shangri-La Dialogue, Singapore, May 30, 2015, https://www.iiss.org/en/events/shangri%20la%20dialogue/archive/shangri-la-dialogue-2015-862b/plenary1-976e/carter-7fa0.

24. Reuters, "Pentagon Chief Pledges $24.2 Million to Hanoi to Buy Patrol Boats," *Straits Times*, May 31, 2015, http://www.straitstimes.com/asia/se-asia/pentagon-chief-pledges-242-million-for-hanoi-to-buy-patrol-boats?page=1.

25. In current U.S. dollars. SIPRI, "SIPRI Military Expenditure Database."

24 destroyers, 49 frigates, 8 corvettes, 85 missile-armed patrol boats, and nearly 60 amphibious ships.[26]

By contrast, Southeast Asian navies operate 15 submarines, 1 small aircraft carrier, no destroyers, 35 frigates, 73 corvettes, and 78 offshore patrol vessels. Many of these vessels are essentially obsolete, particularly those belonging to Myanmar, Indonesia, the Philippines, and Thailand.[27]

In terms of civilian law enforcement vessels, China and the countries of Southeast Asia operate a large number of small vessels for use in coastal waters; they, however, are unsuitable for high-seas operations. As noted earlier, according the U.S. DOD, China has added approximately 50 oceangoing vessels to its coast guard since 2004, while the U.S. Office of Naval Intelligence estimates that China has 95 "large" (over 1,000 tons) patrol boats.[28]

Collectively, the maritime states of Southeast Asia operate only 14 oceangoing coast guard vessels.[29] In contrast, the new China's coast guard vessels are much larger and more heavily armed than their Southeast Asian counterparts. In May 2015, for example, China commissioned the *Zhongguo Haijin* 2901, the first ship in a new class of vessel that, at 10,000 tons displacement, is by far the world's largest coast guard cutter.[30]

In short, Southeast Asian navies and coast guards are veritable minnows when compared to the Chinese whale.

Southeast Asia's Limited Options

Beijing's artificial island building in the South China Sea has triggered a debate in the United States on how best Washington can leverage diplomatic and military tools to deter or even challenge Chinese assertiveness in the maritime domain, especially those actions deemed to infringe freedom of navigation. Still others are beginning to question whether the United States needs to fundamentally rethink its more than four-decade-old policy of "engagement" with China.[31]

---

26. Office of the Secretary of Defense, *Military and Security Developments*, 44.

27. See Thomas Withington and Richard Pain, *Asia OPV and Corvette Market Report 2015* (n.p.: IQPC Global, 2015), http://www.opvscorvettesasia.com/media/1000965/38886.pdf. The author is indebted to Collin Koh Swee Lean of the Rajaratnam School of International Studies in Singapore for additional figures.

28. Office of the Secretary of Defense, *Military and Security Developments*, 44; Office of Naval Intelligence, *The PLA Navy*, 41.

29. Defence iQ, *Global Offshore Patrol Vessels: Market Report 2015–2016* (n.p.: IQPC Global, 2015), http://www.offshorepatrolvessels.com/media/1000900/47110.pdf.

30. Ryan D. Martinson, "East Asian Security in the Age of the Chinese Mega-Cutter," Center for International Maritime Security, July 3, 2015, http://cimsec.org/east-asian-security-age-chinese-mega-cutter/16974.

31. See, for example, Geoff Dyer, "US Struggles for Strategy to Contain China's Island-Building," *Financial Times*, June 8, 2015; Robert A. Manning, "America's 'China Consensus' Implodes," *National Interest*, May 21, 2015; David Feith, "The Great American Rethink on China," *Wall Street Journal*, May 28, 2015.

China's reclamation activities have elicited plenty of concern across Southeast Asia and, unsurprisingly, protests from the Philippines and Vietnam, which have accused China of violating their sovereignty and sovereign rights. Unlike in the United States, however, the reclamation work has not led Southeast Asian governments to fundamentally question their policies toward China. Some countries may recalibrate slightly, such as Malaysia since it has been perturbed by Chinese encroachments in its EEZ over the past few years.

A more robust military posture toward China is, of course, out of the question. Southeast Asian governments are well aware of the growing chasm that has developed between themselves and China in terms of defense spending and military capabilities. They can do little to reduce that chasm, not collectively and certainly not individually.

Southeast Asian states remain committed to expanding trade and investment links with China and engaging it diplomatically, both bilaterally and at the various ASEAN-led multilateral forums such as the ASEAN Regional Forum, ASEAN Plus Three, ASEAN Defense Ministers' Meeting Plus, and the East Asia Summit. Alternative policies are seen as unpalatable, as well as unrealistic and perhaps even counterproductive. With regard to the South China Sea dispute in particular, ASEAN member states remain committed to the two-decade-long conflict management process with China, even as that process seems increasingly irrelevant to events on the water.

Thirteen years after it was signed, none of the joint cooperative measures outlined in the ASEAN-China Declaration on the Conduct of Parties in the South China Sea (DOC) have been implemented. Moreover, China's massive reclamation activities are wholly incompatible with Article 5 of the DOC, which calls on the parties to "exercise self-restrain in the conduct of activities that would complicate or escalate disputes." China's de facto occupation of Scarborough Shoal in 2012 may not have technically violated the clause that calls on the claimants to refrain from occupying uninhabited atolls, but it certainly violates its spirit.

Talks on a binding and comprehensive code of conduct (COC) for the South China Sea between ASEAN and China have been ongoing since 2013. ASEAN leaders and officials have repeatedly called for the talks to be expedited in the hope and expectation that a code might mitigate tensions. Yet, as Le Luong Minh, ASEAN's secretary-general, complained, ASEAN has been unable to engage China in "substantive discussions" on the COC.[32] The speculation all along has been that China seeks to prolong the talks for as long as possible, while at the same time expanding and consolidating its presence within the nine-dash line. The reclamation work tends to reinforce this view.

Ironically China's behavior over the past two years has led to a strengthening of ASEAN unity over the South China Sea. There has been no repeat of the Phnom Penh fiasco of 2012, when disagreements between the ASEAN chair, Cambodia, and the Philippines over

32. Razak Ahmad and Mergawati Zulfakar, "ASEAN Sec-Gen Minh: Urgent to Engage China over Sea Spat," *Star* (Kuala Lumpur), April 26, 2015, http://www.thestar.com.my/News/Nation/2015/04/26/Asean-summit-south-china-sea-spat-dangerous/.

whether the dispute should be mentioned in ASEAN's final communique led to a breakdown in the ASEAN consensus.[33] In fact, since that embarrassing episode, the ASEAN states have, to certain extent, closed ranks.

At the beginning of the Haiyang Shiyou 981 oil rig crisis in 2014, ASEAN issued a standalone statement, at Hanoi's request, that expressed "serious concerns" at developments.[34] In April 2015, under pressure from Manila, ASEAN expressed "serious concerns" at the land reclamation and said that this had "eroded trust and confidence and may undermine peace, security, and stability in the South China Sea."[35] While ASEAN did not name China directly, it was obvious from the word "reclamations" that it was referring to China. It is ASEAN's strongest statement to date on the dispute. Yet despite this recent show of unity, ASEAN state members appear increasingly unable to influence China's behavior, or persuade it that a binding COC is in the interests of regional peace and stability.

That being the case, the ASEAN states, and especially those who have conflicting territorial and maritime boundary claims with China, continue to balance against China, both internally—by modernizing their armed forces to provide a modicum of deterrence—and externally—by supporting the presence of U.S. armed forces, as well as those of other countries.

As China's power rises and it moves to assert dominance within the nine-dash line, the U.S. balancing role becomes more important. Even though as they support and facilitate that presence, to varying degrees, Southeast Asian states worry that if the United States adopts measures to challenge Chinese assertiveness, this will act as a catalyst for strategic rivalry between Washington and Beijing. The South China Sea is currently at the heart of this emerging rivalry. As the dispute worsens, Southeast Asian countries will have to grapple with the serious dilemmas that this will inevitably pose.

33. "S. China Sea Row Forces ASEAN to Forego Communique for 1st Time in 45 Years," *Straits Times*, July 12, 2012, http://www.thefreelibrary.com/UPDATE2%3A+S.+China+Sea+row+forces+ASEAN+to+forego+communique+for+1st...-a0296543592.

34. "ASEAN Foreign Minister's Statement on the Current Developments in the South China Sea," May 10, 2014, http://www.asean.org/news/asean-statement-communiques/item/asean-foreign-ministers-statement-on-the-current-developments-in-the-south-china-sea.

35. "Chairman's Statement of the 26th ASEAN Summit," April 28, 2015, http://www.asean.org/news/asean-statement-communiques/item/chairman-s-statement-of-the-26th-asean-summit.

8 Recent Developments in the South China Sea

A Chinese Perspective

Wu Shicun

This paper will address the following three issues: activities that have considerably influenced the South China Sea situation, China-U.S. relations in the maritime domain, and the author's recommendations for managing the South China Sea situation going forward.

From a Chinese perspective, the current South China Sea situation can be summarized as generally stable and controllable but with growing uncertainty, which can be attributed to various factors. One of the most notable factors has been the land reclamation and feature construction work conducted by disputed countries.

Activities Influencing the South China Sea Situation

The paper will begin by clarifying and explaining China's position and intentions with regards to the reclamation issue. First, compared with countries such as Vietnam and Malaysia, China is a latecomer when it comes to land reclamation in the South China Sea. Second, China's construction will not change the legal nature of the insular features. Third, China needs to protect its legitimate rights in these waters. For this purpose, China's reclamation work in the South China Sea is aimed at improving China's capacity to deliver maritime public services, maintaining maritime safety and security, offering support to search and rescue operations and scientific research, and improving the living and working conditions of fishermen and other people stationed on the islands and reefs. These objectives befit China's international and regional responsibility as a big country. Therefore, China's construction work in the South China Sea should be treated objectively, constructively, and fairly.

The second driver behind rising tensions in the South China Sea is U.S. surveillance and patrol activities near the Spratly Islands. On May 14, 2015, the U.S Navy announced that the littoral combat ship USS *Fort Worth* had arrived for resupply in the Philippines after completing a week-long patrol in the South China Sea, which took it near the disputed Spratly Islands. Later in that month, a U.S. Navy P-8 Poseidon surveillance aircraft flew directly over a Chinese-administered artificial island constructed atop the Fiery Cross Reef in the South China Sea. At the Shangri-La Dialogue in Singapore in May, U.S. defense secretary Ashton Carter also pledged that the United States would maintain a substantial presence in the region and "will fly, sail, and operate wherever international law allows."[1]

These U.S. activities were to a large extent responsible for the escalation of tension in the South China Sea. The United States conflates these intelligence, surveillance, and reconnaissance activities with commercial navigation. As a matter of fact, China has no interest in obstructing commercial shipping or flights across the South China Sea, but does object to what it perceives as the U.S. abuse of its rights to freedom of navigation.

The third aspect influencing the current South China Sea situation is related to activities conducted by extra-regional powers. Besides the United States, Japan has also shown great interest in asserting itself in the South China Sea as a way to boost its regional military presence. This is exemplified by the revision of guidelines for U.S.-Japan defense cooperation and the newly passed security bills in Japan's Lower House of Parliament that, if approved by the upper chamber, would see Japan deploy forces abroad to assist its allies.

The United States has also strengthened its alliance with the Philippines and military cooperation with Vietnam. This indicates that the United States aims at fencing China for its own strategic purposes, and has shifted away from its previous commitment to stay neutral and not take sides in the South China Sea dispute. This policy shift has served as a strategic incentive for other extra-regional powers such as Japan to intervene in the South China Sea affairs, further complicating the disputes and regional situation.

The fourth aspect is related to unilateral activities by some claimant countries. The Philippines, which has also reclaimed and built on features and exploited oil resources in disputed areas, decided to unilaterally launch an arbitration against China. This unilateral bid for arbitration will not help solve the dispute between the Philippines and China. Any third party that does not adequately understand the context, including international judicial and arbitration organs, cannot help the two countries find a real solution to the dispute. This case is not only in contravention of relevant bilateral agreements, but is also not conducive to building trust between the two countries going forward.

Lastly, the consultation process for a code of conduct (COC) in the South China Sea is progressing slowly. Since the signing of the Declaration on the Conduct of Parties in the South China Sea in 2002, there have been very few bilateral or multilateral cooperative

1. Ashton Carter, "The United States and Challenges of Asia-Pacific Security," Speech at 14th IISS [International Institute for Strategic Studies] Asia Security Summit/Shangri-La Dialogue, Singapore, May 30, 2015), https://www.iiss.org/en/events/shangri%20la%20dialogue/archive/shangri-la-dialogue-2015-862b/plenary1-976e/carter-7fa0.

projects taking place in the South China Sea. Hence, it will likely take a fairly long time to conclude the COC because of the complexities of the issues and different intentions of countries involved. Having said that, China will continue to work together with Association of Southeast Asian States (ASEAN) states to achieve this.

China-U.S. Relations in the Maritime Domain

Despite the divergent perceptions between the United States and China, both countries share many common interests in the maritime domain, as indicated by the various existing cooperation mechanisms. Three agreements were achieved between the two governments in 2014 alone.

In April 2014 naval chiefs from over 20 countries in the Asia Pacific, including those of the United States and China, endorsed the Code for Unplanned Encounters at Sea (CUES) at the Western Pacific Naval Symposium in Qingdao, China. The CUES proposes regulations on the legal status, rights, and obligations for naval warships and aircraft, and prescribes maritime safety and communication procedures in case of unplanned encounters at sea. In November China and the United States reached two memoranda of understanding on naval and air military encounters and notification for major military activities between the two sides. This confidence-building mechanism urges both the Chinese and U.S. militaries to push defense cooperation and mutual trust to a new level, handle differences properly, and identify potential flashpoints for conflict.

More recently, during the seventh China-U.S. Strategic and Economic Dialogue in Washington in late June 2015, officials from both sides again placed emphasis on cooperation. John Kerry, U.S. secretary of state, called on countries with competing claims to "exercise restraint, refrain from unilateral actions, and settle their differences in accordance with international law."[2] Yang Jiechi, Chinese state councilor, suggested promoting maritime research, development, maintenance, and protection, citing the increased maritime policy exchanges and practical cooperation between the two militaries. Such high-level consensus can facilitate practical maritime cooperation between the two countries within the framework of international institutions and law.

These actions are significant milestones in confidence-building measures and forging mutual trust, signaling both sides' determination to promote what President Xi Jinping calls a "new type of military relations."[3] Nevertheless, China and the United States should go beyond these existing mechanisms and further improve bilateral defense cooperation.

---

2. U.S. Department of State, "The Strategic and Economic Dialogue: Consultation on People-to-People Exchange Closing Statements," June 24, 2015, http://www.state.gov/secretary/remarks/2015/06/244208.htm.
3. "President Xi Advocates New Type of Military Relations with U.S.," Xinhua, November 12, 2014, http://news.xinhuanet.com/english/china/2014-11/12/c_133784921.htm.

Recommendations

The following are four recommendations on how to better manage the South China Sea situation in general. First, the United States and China should recognize that mutual respect is fundamental to any aspect of bilateral relations and acknowledge the legitimate interests of each other. For the United States, a balanced policy in the South China Sea can alleviate China's concerns about being contained in the region. For China, the reclaimed features should be used mainly for civilian purposes, and military facilities on these features should not go beyond defensive needs. In addition, China should make earnest efforts to promote the consultation on the COC in the South China Sea.

Second, it is time to initiate a regional mechanism on the consultation of maritime affairs between China and the United States, in line with the safety and security of navigation and in order to reduce the risk of incidents at sea. This rules-based mechanism could be the most effective measure to promote confidence building and crisis management, enhance mutual understanding, and ease regional tensions.

Third, Japan should not interfere in the South China Sea because it is a non-party to the dispute. Japan recently has been deliberating whether to become more involved with the issue. If it does, Japanese involvement will likely only stir up conflicts among regional countries and create further tensions at sea. Japan can neither contribute to the resolution of the dispute nor protect peace and stability in the South China Sea. Washington should not encourage Tokyo to conduct or join the United States in its patrol activities in the South China Sea.

Finally, China and the United States can work through their issues together. The South China Sea is important to both, if sometimes for different reasons. It is, however, in both nations' interests that the sea remains a calm avenue for global shipping. The two countries should not let their differences divide them, but should instead let similarities lead toward a common future.

About the Editors and Contributors

Renato Cruz de Castro is a professor in the International Studies Department at De La Salle University, Manila, and the holder of the Charles Lui Chi Keung Professorial Chair in China Studies. He was previously the U.S. State Department ASEAN Research Fellow from the Philippines, and in 2009 he was with the Political Science Department of Arizona State University. His research interests include Philippine-U.S. security relations, Philippine defense and foreign policy, U.S. defense and foreign policy in East Asia, and the politics of East Asia. Professor de Castro earned his doctorate degree from the Government and International Studies Department of the University of South Carolina as a Fulbright Scholar in 2011.

Patrick M. Cronin is a senior adviser and senior director of the Asia-Pacific Security Program at the Center for a New American Security. Previously he was the senior director of the Institute for National Strategic Studies (INSS) at the National Defense University, where he simultaneously oversaw the Center for the Study of Chinese Military Affairs. Dr. Cronin has a diverse background in Asia-Pacific security and U.S. defense, foreign, and development policy. Prior to leading INSS he served as the director of studies at the London-based International Institute for Strategic Studies (IISS). At the IISS he also served as editor of the Adelphi Papers and as executive director of the Armed Conflict Database. Before joining IISS Dr. Cronin was senior vice president and director of research at CSIS.

Bonnie S. Glaser is senior adviser for Asia in the Freeman Chair in China Studies at CSIS, where she works on issues related to Chinese foreign and security policy. She is also a senior associate with CSIS Pacific Forum and a consultant for the U.S. government on East Asia. From 2003 to mid-2008 Ms. Glaser was a senior associate in the CSIS International Security Program. Prior to joining CSIS she served as a consultant for various U.S. government offices, including the Departments of Defense and State. She has written extensively on Chinese threat perceptions and views of the strategic environment, China's foreign policy, Sino-U.S. relations, U.S.-China military ties, cross-strait relations, Chinese assessments of the Korean peninsula, and Chinese perspectives on missile defense and multilateral security in Asia.

Bill Hayton spent a year (2006–2007) as a BBC reporter in Vietnam and then wrote *Vietnam: Rising Dragon* (Yale University Press, 2010). In 2011 he began writing *The South China Sea: The Struggle for Power in Asia* (Yale University Press, 2014), which was completed during 2013 while he was working in Myanmar. He has worked for BBC News since 1998 and currently works for BBC World News TV. In the past Hayton has worked in the World Service (Radio) Newsroom, on Radio News Programs, and with the European language services. Before joining the BBC he freelanced for several years at APTN, CNBC, European Business News, and Sky News.

Murray Hiebert serves as senior fellow and deputy director of the Sumitro Chair for Southeast Asia Studies at CSIS. Prior to joining CSIS he was senior director for Southeast Asia at the U.S. Chamber of Commerce, where he worked to promote trade and investment opportunities between the United States and Asia. Mr. Hiebert joined the Chamber of Commerce in 2006 from the *Wall Street Journal*'s China bureau. Prior to his Beijing posting he worked for the *Wall Street Journal Asia* and the *Far Eastern Economic Review* in Washington and before that for the *Far Eastern Economic Review* in Bangkok, Hanoi, and Kuala Lumpur. Mr. Hiebert is the author of two books on Vietnam, *Chasing the Tigers* (Kodansha, 1996) and *Vietnam Notebook* (Review Publishing, 1993).

Peter Jennings commenced as executive director of the Australian Strategic Policy Institute on April 30, 2012. Prior to that he was the deputy secretary for strategy in the Australian Department of Defence. Mr. Jennings's career has included extensive experience advising government at senior levels, developing major strategic policy documents, conducting crisis management, and researching, writing, and teaching international security. He previously held a number of first assistant secretary positions in the Department of Defence, including the International Policy Division and Coordination and Public Affairs office; he was also secretary of the Defence Audit and Risk Committee.

Phuong Nguyen is a research associate with the Sumitro Chair for Southeast Asia Studies at CSIS. She conducts research and writes on Southeast Asia, U.S. foreign policy toward the countries in the Association of Southeast Asian Nations (ASEAN), and China's peripheral diplomacy. She is the coauthor of a number of works, including most recently *Building a More Robust U.S.-Philippines Alliance* (CSIS, August 2015) and *Southeast Asia's Geopolitical Centrality and the U.S.-Japan Alliance* (CSIS, June 2015). She holds an MA in Asian studies from the School of International Service at American University in Washington, D.C.

Pham Lan Dung is the dean of International Law Faculty and acting director general of the Diplomatic Academy of Vietnam (DAV) in Hanoi. Her main duties include training, researching, advising in international law, and other tasks assigned by the Ministry of Foreign Affairs of Vietnam. She teaches courses in public international law, the law of treaties, legal aspects of international organizations, constitutional law, and intellectual property law. She received her diploma from Moscow State Institute of International Relations in 1993, her MALD from the Fletcher School of Law and Diplomacy in 2002, and her PhD from DAV in 2014.

Gregory B. Poling is director of the Asia Maritime Transparency Initiative and a fellow with the Sumitro Chair for Southeast Asia Studies at CSIS. His research interests include disputes in the South China Sea, democratization in Southeast Asia, and Asian multilateralism. Mr. Poling is the author of *The South China Sea in Focus: Clarifying the Limits of*

Maritime Dispute (CSIS, 2015) and coauthor of a number of works, including most recently *Building a More Robust U.S.-Philippines Alliance* (CSIS, 2015). He received an MA in international affairs from American University and a BA in history and philosophy from Saint Mary's College of Maryland, and he studied at Fudan University in Shanghai.

Ian Storey is a senior fellow at the Institute of Southeast Asian Studies (ISEAS) in Singapore. He specializes in Asian security issues, with a focus on Southeast Asia. At ISEAS he is the editor *Contemporary Southeast Asia*, a peer-reviewed academic journal. His research interests include Southeast Asia's relations with China, the United States, and Japan; maritime security in the Asia Pacific (especially the South China Sea dispute); and China's foreign and defense policies. Prior to joining ISEAS he held academic positions at the U.S. Defense Department's Asia-Pacific Center for Security Studies in Honolulu, Hawaii, and at Deakin University in Melbourne, Australia. He received his PhD from the City University of Hong Kong.

Tran Huu Duy Minh is a lecturer on the International Law Faculty at the Diplomatic Academy of Vietnam in Hanoi. His research interests include the law of the sea, the law of treaties, and the settlement of international disputes.

Wu Shicun is president and senior research fellow of the National Institute for South China Sea Studies and deputy director of the Collaborative Innovation Center of South China Sea Studies at Nanjing University. His research interests cover the history and geography of the South China Sea, maritime delimitation, maritime economy, international relations, and regional security strategy. His books include *Solving Disputes for Regional Cooperation and Development in the South China Sea: A Chinese Perspective* (Chandos, 2013), *A Study on the South China Sea Disputes* (Hainan, 2005), and *The Origin and Development of the Nansha Disputes* (Ocean Press, 1999). Wu has published widely in academic journals. He has been interviewed frequently in the media about South China Sea issues.

www.ingramcontent.com/pod-product-compliance
Ingram Content Group UK Ltd.
Pitfield, Milton Keynes, MK11 3LW, UK
UKHW051419150926
475561UK00005B/241

9 781442 258945